YOU
ARE
WHAT
YOU
THINK

Other Books by David Stoop

The Angry Man

Forgiving Our Parents, Forgiving Ourselves: Healing Adult Children of Dysfunctional Families, 2nd ed.

Hope for the Perfectionist

The Intimacy Factor

The Life Recovery Devotional

Making Peace with Your Father

Saying Goodbye to Disappointments

What's He So Angry About?

YOU ARE WHAT YOU THINK

Using Positive Self-Talk to Change Your Life

Dr. David Stoop

Revell

a division of Baker Publishing Group
Grand Rapids, Michigan

© 1982, 1996 by David Stoop

Published by Revell
a division of Baker Publishing Group
P.O. Box 6287, Grand Rapids, MI 49516-6287
www.revellbooks.com

Paperback edition published 2017

Previously published in 1982 and 1996 under the title *Self-Talk: Key to Personal Growth*

Printed in the United States of America

Library of Congress Cataloging-in-Publication Data for the previous edition is on file at the Library of Congress, Washington, DC.

ISBN 978-0-8007-2836-6

Unless otherwise indicated, Scripture quotations are from the Revised Standard Version of the Bible, copyright 1952 [2nd edition, 1971] by the Division of Christian Education of the National Council of the Churches of Christ in the United States of America. Used by permission. All rights reserved..

Scripture marked TLB is taken from The Living Bible © 1971. Used by permission of Tyndale House Publishers, Inc., Carol Stream, Illinois 60188. All rights reserved.

Scripture marked KJV is taken from the King James Version of the Bible.

Scripture marked PHILLIPS is taken from The New Testament in Modern English, revised edition—J. B. Phillips, translator. © J. B. Phillips 1958, 1960, 1972. Used by permission of Macmillan Publishing Co., Inc.

The cartoon on page 133 is © 1979 by the Universal Press Syndicate. All rights reserved.

17   18   19   20   21   22   23   7   6   5   4   3

It is to Jan, with love,
that I dedicate "our" book

Contents

ONE

The Search
for Self-Control

A man without self-control is as defenseless as a city with
broken-down walls.

Proverbs 25:28 TLB

Attitude is everything!" Every motivational speaker underlines that
message. All coaches hammer that truth home to their players.
Anyone working with other people knows how important attitude
is in determining the successful outcome of any task. The apostle
Paul emphasized the importance of our attitude when he wrote,
"Now your attitudes and thoughts must all be constantly changing
for the better" (Eph. 4:23 TLB).

The importance of attitude seems so clear to us when we look
at other people. How often do we think or say about one of our
children or our husband or wife, "They have an attitude problem!"
We see people who have the greatest intentions and whose motives

are spiritually and morally sound but who cannot succeed because their attitude is negative and self-critical.

Paradoxically, we want God's very best for ourselves and our relationships. We have right and good intentions; and we prayerfully and thoughtfully set goals for ourselves. But then we fall again and again into the same routines and patterns of behavior that keep us right where we've always been—where we don't want to be. Experience has proven over and over that good intentions and the best goal-setting skills simply aren't enough.

Knowledge is never enough either. Lots of people have all kinds of impressive credentials and have accumulated volumes of important knowledge and skills, but they have never really been able to get their lives moving in any direction. We look at them and shake our heads, thinking of all that wasted potential, and wonder why they put all that effort into "getting ready" when it appears to everyone watching that they don't intend to ever "get started."

The one thing, from a human perspective, that seems to make the difference between those who succeed and those who fail is attitude. No matter who you are, attitude really is everything—it's what makes the difference in every aspect of life.

OK, but even if we agree that attitude is everything, it still sounds so superficial. "When I face a problem," we protest, "I immediately want to work on my goals or on expanding my knowledge base. It can't be as simple as changing my attitude!" What we can so clearly see as the issue in someone else just doesn't seem to be that evident, or important, when we look at ourselves. Perhaps it's because our own attitudes are so much a part of us that we really can't identify them. Or if and when we do recognize a problem with our attitude, it just frustrates us because we don't know how to change it.

Our World Feels Out of Control

All too often our attitudes are the by-product of our experiences in an out-of-control world. And when pressed to change our attitudes, our internal response may be, "How? I feel so helpless, so out of control!" And really, how can a person feel in control when the newspapers confront us every day with increasing evidence that the world *out there* is out of control? Prices soar unchecked. The national debt reaches beyond the incomprehensible figure of a trillion dollars. The environment is rapidly being depleted of its resources. The air is polluted, water is contaminated, and our food increasingly needs enrichment.

But the evidence of an outer world beyond our control pales in significance when compared to our inner feelings of not being able to control our own personal lives. Every day I encounter this in my work with people.

Families are out of control. Divorces have outnumbered marriages for several years. Young adults shy away from marriage on the premise that they can't find any examples of happily married couples. Children from fractured homes feel divided and powerless—how can a child possibly keep track of four sets of grandparents and all the step-relationships within an ever-changing family structure? Too many children grow up in a chaotic world and know they are out of control.

How do kids cope with these feelings? Many, sadly, slip into the drug culture. The statistics are frightening. Did you know that the money generated through the sale of drugs tops that of even our country's largest corporations?

Because of the chaos and stress, many of us end up not feeling well. Over 40 million Americans suffer from allergies; and 30 million suffer from sleep-onset insomnia. It's estimated that 25 million people in the United States are afflicted with hypertension (high blood pressure). Around 20 million of us have ulcers, and too many millions suffer from jagged nerves to the point of needing tranquilizers. And more than that, one out of three persons has a weight problem, creating unhealthy cycles of weight loss and gain.

Health specialists used to argue over which diseases could be classified as psychosomatic (beginning in the mind). Today most medical research indicates that between 75 and 90 percent of all illness is caused by the stresses of modern life. In fact, many researchers no longer ask *which* diseases are stress related; instead, they ask how much of *every* disease is stress related.

We can numb our pain, distract ourselves from it, project it, and try to deny it's even there; but none of these escapes can truly relieve our pain. Only an honest understanding of ourselves and our God can do that.

Understanding Our Emotions

Psychologists have traditionally agreed that we all experience three basic emotions: love, anger, and fear. We can liken these to the three primary colors: red, yellow, and blue. Every color, shade, and hue we see is one of these three primary colors or some combination of them. In the same way, every feeling we experience in life is one of the primary emotions or, more likely, some combination of them.

To better understand the three primary emotions, it helps to see that each one has movement and direction. Love is the emotion that always moves us *toward* someone or something. When I love someone, I want to be with that person. I move toward him or her. I want to hear his or her voice and feel his or her touch. If I am in love with something—for example, chocolate—I find that I always end up at the candy store whenever I go to the mall. Love for chocolate draws me there, and I may not even be aware of it until my senses tell me I am there.

The movement of anger is not only toward but also *against* someone or something. Anger is a separating emotion. I move toward the object of my anger, but with a marked intensity that either strikes out against that object or pushes it away.

The movement of fear is always *away* from someone or something. If I am afraid, I back away. I want to get away from the object of my fear. If I am afraid to ride in elevators, I keep my distance from them. If I am afraid of confrontation, I will back away from the person involved and avoid any possible conflict with him or her.

Anger and fear, emotions that are opposite in direction, have been called the emotions that trigger the fight/flight syndrome. Anger prepares me to fight—to move against and push away. Fear prepares me to take flight—to move away from the threat. Both anger and fear are reactions to a threat. Interestingly, what takes place physiologically (in my body) when I am angry is identical to what happens when I am fearful. The difference is in my perception of the threat—how I see that which is threatening me.

For example, let's say you are visiting a friend of yours in a distant city. He lives in a part of the town that seems scary and dangerous to you. One evening you borrow his car and return to his home quite late. You can find a parking space only several blocks away.

As you lock the car and start walking toward your friend's house, you hear footsteps behind you. You momentarily slow down; so do the footsteps. You speed up; so do they. You start running; so do they. What would any normal human being experience in that situation? Fear! Lots of it!

You run toward your friend's house, but just as you get the key in the door, the footsteps come up behind you and stop. A voice behind you says, "Ha! I gotcha!" You turn around and see that the footsteps belong to your friend. Now what do you feel? Anger! Instantly!

What happened? For one thing, your emotions changed from fear to anger in a split second. And the reason they did is based on the other thing that changed—your perception of the threat. When the threat was the unknown, the pursuing footsteps, you imagined all kinds of horrible things that could happen if your pursuer caught up with you. When the threat became known and was seen to no longer be a threat, anger became the natural response.

If that friend is also your fiancé, you can see how the three primary emotions of love, anger, and fear can get all mixed up, and we can move from love to fear to anger—and back and forth between them—in a confusing pattern.

When we add to these three emotions the myriad of feelings we experience, it gets even more complex. We use the term *feelings* to describe worry, guilt, anxiety, sadness, depression, happiness, joy, contentment, and so forth. But I can better understand this myriad of feelings if I can understand the three basic emotions and how they work. My understanding of their movement will also help me sort out what I am experiencing emotionally when I am in a sequence of events like those described above that have all three emotions working at the same time.

Another important point to understand about the three basic emotions is how they are related to self-control. The emotions of anger and fear are reactions to threatening situations or people. Love is the emotion of self-control, for when love is our response, we are able to act, not react, to life.

Overwhelmed or Overcontrolling

We respond in one of two ways when we are confused by our feelings and emotions. We either become overwhelmed, allowing our feelings to spill over onto those around us and draw them into a confusing drama; or we become overcontrolling, holding a tight rein on any expression of our feelings or emotions while also attempting to carefully control everything that goes on around us.

When we are overwhelmed by our world, we retreat into something that appears safe—a place to hide. But we soon discover that we are still out of control and need to find new places to hide or new ways to escape.

Marge is a good example of someone overwhelmed by life. She's friendly and caring, always taking the time to listen to her friend's problems. But lately she finds herself drained by the experience. As she lies awake at night, unable to sleep, her mind races back over all the things she needed to get done that day but didn't. Or she lies there wrestling with possible solutions to help her friend. Anything but sleep.

When she drags herself out of bed in the morning, she's confronted with yesterday's dirty dishes—plus a few from the day before. The pile of dirty clothes seems to touch the ceiling. And then the phone starts to ring. In between calls Marge collapses on the sofa, paralyzed by the thought of all that needs to be done. Or in desperation she heads out to the shopping mall just to try to get away from everyone and everything.

When she tries to discipline her kids, they use a variety of ways to distract her attention until she finally gives in, throwing her hands up in despair. Her kids learned long ago how to hook into her feeling of being overwhelmed and work it to their advantage.

Marge's craft room spills over into other rooms in the house. She's interested in different projects, starting them with enthusiasm but seldom seeing anything through to completion. She wishes she weren't such a procrastinator.

Occasionally Marge gets her work all caught up and feels a degree of control over her life. She vows never to let things get out of control again—a vow that is usually broken in a couple of days. She longs for an effective way to organize her life, but she doesn't have any idea how to begin.

Sometimes the feeling of being overwhelmed takes the form of a phobia, as in Donna's case. She is afraid of crowds, afraid of heights, and afraid of being closed in. When she first came to my office, she sat on the edge of the couch with her eyes glued to the door. As we talked she related how her fears had recently intensified.

Usually her family adapts to her phobias. They know they will have to arrive at church late so she can stand in the back near the door. They also know they will leave early so Donna can avoid having to talk with anyone.

Her husband, Fred, doesn't schedule many social commitments. When he must, Donna has to ensure her safety with the same tactic—arrive late and leave early. Lately they have had to leave several social engagements earlier than planned, for Donna has experienced anxiety attacks that included fainting spells.

Her phobias appear to be aggravated by Fred's upcoming promotion to head up his company's new plant. Donna's phobias no longer appear to be a safe place for her to hide, for Fred's new position will make new and threatening demands on her.

Inside, Donna's emotions rage like a hurricane. She obviously doesn't faint on purpose. And she really can't control her phobias. Every time she tries to socialize, her anxiety attacks get worse. She is overwhelmed by emotions and feelings she can't even begin to understand. Her family's empathy only adds feelings of guilt to her fears.

Marge and Donna are examples of two people overwhelmed by emotions and feelings. From outward appearances you might not recognize that either of them is out of control. But inside, their emotions and feelings swing violently, adding to their fears and feelings of frustration.

The other response, becoming overcontrolling, can be just as devastating. But overcontrolling people are even better at hiding the conflict. This method of coping leads such people to push themselves and to push those around them. And they will push until something snaps, usually their health. Then they are even more out of control.

Peggy is an expert at overcontrolling her emotions. Her attempts at control push her to the point of feeling as though she will explode. But outwardly Peggy is regarded as Mrs. Efficient! Her home is always spotless, even though she would be quick to point out the less-than-perfect spot. Her meals are always on time and look as though a dietitian planned them. Younger mothers and wives look at Peggy with feelings of awe and envy. Everything she does is done well. And she stays so busy that she wears everyone else out just watching her.

Everyone in the family toes the line. Her kids are afraid to step out of line for fear of being put on restriction. Whenever they try to protest, they are put into a "lose" position and forced to retreat. Even her husband seems to be afraid to challenge her routine. So he quietly fits into Peggy's scheduling of the household.

Underneath the surface, though, Peggy is a churning sea of questions and self-doubt. She wonders if she can do anything right. She's never satisfied with the way her house looks, the way the kids behave, or the way her life is headed. Sometimes she wishes she could die so she could relieve her family of the burden she feels she is to them. Suicide often appears to her to be the only way she can escape the responsibilities of her life.

But Peggy presses on. She must not let up. So she dutifully structures every moment of every day. And if anyone fails to keep to her schedule or causes her to change it, she feels as if her whole world is threatened. And it is, for any change brings with it the possibility that she will lose control. And that she can't afford to do!

Arnie also overcontrols his life in an effort to retain control. Lately his wife has really been on his case. Her latest effort was to threaten separation if he didn't agree to counseling. As far as he's concerned, everything's fine. It's his wife who has the problem. "I'm only here because she needs help," he insisted. After a couple of frustrating sessions, I asked Arnie to come in for some sessions alone. Gradually the following facts began to emerge.

Arnie is having a tough time at work. His boss has been putting a lot of pressure on him because his sales are down, and Arnie doesn't need the added pressure from his wife right now. He sincerely seems to feel that everything in the marriage is fine, suggesting his wife's problem might be due to the beginning of menopause.

Only once in nearly four hours of conversation did Arnie show even the slightest hint of any feelings. While talking about his oldest son, Arnie had to stop for a few moments in order to regain control of his emotions. His son is a disappointment. He left home when he was seventeen, and Arnie and his wife haven't heard from him in five years. His lips quivered as he shared that information, and his eyes seemed to cloud. But in a few moments Arnie had everything back under control and was ready to talk about anything—except his son.

All through the conversation Arnie had a smile on his face. "Nothing wrong with me that I can't take care of," he asserted. Then he added, "You just help my wife get herself back together. She's the one with problems." He has it all under control—everything but his son and his ulcer. Arnie insists the ulcer came with the job. No one could convince him that it came with the way he handled his emotions.

Arnie and Peggy manage to cope with their world by overcontrolling their emotions. But they walk a tightrope. There is always the possibility that something will push them off and they will lose control. Their solution is simply to expand the areas they control, including everyone around them.

Another way to look at these two basic attempts to retain control of our lives is to imagine ourselves driving a special car. Only we know how to drive it. As we travel down the highway, we suddenly feel overwhelmed, so we decide to put the car into cruise control and jump into the backseat. Then we yell at God, our spouse, our children, our parents, or all of the above. "You take over! I can't drive anymore!"

As the car goes careening down the highway, hitting other cars, running over other people, and bouncing off buildings, we sit there in a panic, saying, "Somebody better get control of this thing!" Perhaps God is sitting with us in the backseat. But all he can say is, "I can't help you back here!" And he explains, "I can't do anything as long as you are sitting in the backseat. I can only help if you're in the driver's seat—if *you* are in control."

If we are overcontrolling, we do just the opposite. We *never* leave the driver's seat. But as we drive along, God, or whoever is close to us, suggests we stop or slow down. But instead we panic and hit the gas pedal, swerving to avoid a collision. Or if we need to turn left, we freeze and our arms become like cement. We can't turn, so we end up hitting the brick wall.

The only way to drive the car is to remain in control. That way if someone with us suggests we slow down, we can slow down. If we need to make a turn, we are not only aware of the directions given to us, we can make the turn. That's self-control. That's the way we are meant to live: exercising self-control in order to be in control! But something's gone wrong; it's not working that way.

Over the years, I've heard many Bible studies and sermons about allowing God to take control of our lives. For many listeners, that's like telling the overwhelmed person in the backseat to let God drive the car. We've already seen that God can't when we won't. Or it's like telling the overcontrolling person to listen to the directions. He can't—he's panicked. Few of those sermons or studies ever point out that God cannot take control of someone who is out of control. That's why we are so often frustrated in our attempts to let God guide us. If we're out of control, we place ourselves beyond the help God wants to give.

One of the basic points in the New Testament is that the follower of Christ is to exercise self-control. In Galatians 5:23 Paul lists self-control as one of the fruits of the Spirit. Being in control—self-control—is the way God means life to be lived. That's why we long to regain control in an out-of-control world.

The reference to Proverbs 25:28 at the beginning of this chapter tells us that "a man without self-control is as defenseless as a city with broken-down walls" (TLB). All through history a city's survival often depended on the strength of its walls. The Israelites knew that fact when they saw Jericho. They looked at those huge walls and thought that city to be secure against their efforts. But God brought the walls tumbling down, and without them, Jericho was defenseless.

I remember visiting the city of Quebec, Canada. I was fascinated by the old section of the city contained within a massive wall. Quebec is the only walled city in North America. As I stood on the top of the wall overlooking the Saint Lawrence River, I remembered some of the history of that place.

During the American Revolution, the American troops chased after the British army. They marched through upstate New York and on into Canada. The British reached Quebec and stopped there. In the battle that followed, the Americans failed miserably, returning home defeated. The reason—Quebec was a walled city. The Americans couldn't penetrate the walls, and the British, inside the walls, successfully defended the city. The walls were a good defense.

This book is about how to get in control of your life. Obviously you can't change everything in your world. What you can do is look for weaknesses in your "walls" and then build a strategy for self-control. Which style of coping do you use when the pressure mounts and you feel control slipping through your fingers? Do you tend to overcontrol or be overwhelmed?

Coping-Style Questionnaire

To help you identify your coping style, let this short questionnaire guide you in discovering how you respond to out-of-control feelings. Now it doesn't just identify weaknesses; it identifies positive things about your style too. The nine items are adapted from an extensive personality test, and there are no right or wrong answers. Respond to each item as quickly as you can. Mark the answer that represents the way you feel most of the time or that represents what feels most comfortable for you.

Coping-Style Questionnaire

		A	B
1. I usually prefer to		☐	☐
	(A) take time to list the things to be done.		
	(B) just plunge in.		
2. I usually		☐	☐
	(A) find waiting to the last minute nerve-racking.		
	(B) prefer to do things at the last minute.		
3. The word that appeals to me the most is		☐	☐
	(A) orderly.		
	(B) easy going.		

4. I am bothered more by ☐ ☐
   (A) constant change.
   (B) routine.

5. I am more comfortable when ☐ ☐
   (A) dates, parties, events are planned far ahead.
   (B) I am free to do whatever comes up.

6. Following a schedule ☐ ☐
   (A) appeals to me.
   (B) cramps my style.

7. I am challenged more by ☐ ☐
   (A) facing something unexpected and quickly seeing what
       must be done.
   (B) following a careful plan to its conclusion.

8. I am generally more ☐ ☐
   (A) systematic.
   (B) casual.

9. I am more ☐ ☐
   (A) punctual.
   (B) leisurely.

Total answers for A and B ☐ ☐

Now count the number of answers you have marked *A* and enter that number in the box below the *A*s. Then count the number of answers you have marked *B* and enter that number in the box under the *B*s. To help you see how strong your tendency is one way or the other, place an *X* on the line below at the point that represents your score. For example, if you had six answers for *A* and three answers for *B*, then put an *X* at that point on the line. See next page.

If your scores are to the right of the center line, then you tend to prefer to keep your options open. You are more comfortable before a decision is made, sometimes even resisting making a decision. You seem to have a play ethic about life. You can postpone work in order to enjoy some other activity or simply to rest. You're a treasure

		Decisive/Orderly					Spontaneous/Flexible			
				X						
A =	9	8	7	6	5	4	3	2	1	0
B =	0	1	2	3	4	5	6	7	8	9

hunter, always looking for what might happen. When faced with deadlines, you may set some artificial ones earlier in order to put some pressure on, but usually you wait until the last minute and then work like crazy. You are more interested in the process that leads to a result than in the result itself.

If you're on the left side of the center line, you are more comfortable after a decision is made. You like things to be fixed and settled. You must work before you can play. So you have a strong emphasis on finishing a task. You like things planned, completed. You want to get the show on the road. Deadlines are serious to your type of person, so you usually plan your work in order to be finished in plenty of time.

People on the left side of the line look at people on the right side and say to them, "You are indecisive, a procrastinator, and you don't have any purpose in life except to mess around!" The people on the right side of the line look at those on the left side and counter, "You are driven and driving, much too task oriented, and you make decisions too quickly!"

Yet being on either side of the line is OK! That's the way you are made. That's your comfort zone. Of course, with every strength there is usually a corresponding weakness. And both sides of the line have weaknesses.

Spontaneous/Flexible people are the ones with the tendency to become overwhelmed and buried by the pressures of life. Because there are so many things they would like to do at any given point in time, they will often postpone mowing the lawn. Then when they see how much the grass has grown, they experience that overwhelmed feeling. Because they often wait too long, they are overwhelmed by the scope of the task and the time available. Donna and Marge would probably score on this side of the line. Marge's score might be eight answers for B and one answer for A. Donna's score might be closer to the center.

Decisive/Orderly people are subject to the tendency to over-control, to become compulsive and harried about life. They always look for the right outcome to every event. When they have a day off, they have to work furiously to get all the odd jobs done before they can relax and enjoy the day. They are usually concerned that everyone else in the family gets his or her work done as well. Urgency is their watchword, and overcontrolling is their weakness. Peggy and Arnie are both examples of people on this side of the scale. Arnie might score something like nine answers for A and no answers for B. Peggy's score wouldn't be as pronounced; perhaps she would answer seven statements for A and two for B.

Another way to look at these two types of coping styles would be to say that Spontaneous/Flexible people are strong in the art of celebrating life and weak in the area of self-discipline. They are good at enjoying life but weak in the area of ordering it.

Decisive/Orderly people can be described as strong in self-discipline but uncomfortable with the art of celebrating life. When they participate in the celebrations of life, such as holidays and special events, everything must follow a schedule; they become uncomfortable with the unexpected. These two patterns of coping can be shown on a grid.

Because overwhelmed people are accepting of their emotions but lack the self-discipline to experience self-control, they often find themselves in the upper left-hand portion of the grid along with Donna and Marge. They experience these overwhelmed feelings

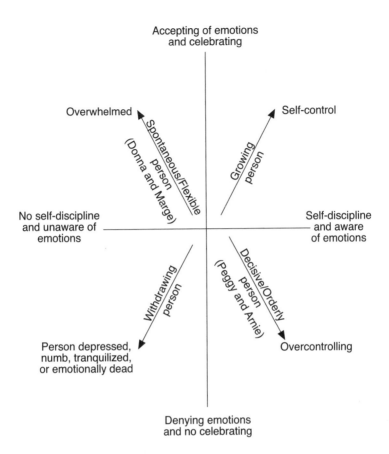

because they are caught in a conflict between emotions they are accepting but are unaware of. They ignore these emotions until it is too late—and they're overwhelmed! Both Donna and Marge are aware of their emotions. Donna knows she has phobias. But they catch her unaware and then overwhelm her. When she has an anxiety attack, it's too late. She's already overwhelmed.

At the opposite corner of the grid, overcontrolling people are aware of certain feelings and emotions, but they want to deny these feelings and emotions. In order to do that, they overcontrol everything that's going on around them. Arnie obviously knows he has strong feelings about his son, but he works hard at denying these feelings. He is certain that if he accepts the reality of these feelings, he will lose control. So he works hard at maintaining a cool, detached outlook on life that is forced to deny any feelings or emotions.

The bottom left corner of the grid is reserved for those who try to escape life by remaining unaware of any emotions and denying the possible existence of these feelings. Usually they can accomplish this only by withdrawing from life through some form of drug or alcohol abuse, developing psychosis, or sinking into a lifestyle of victimization. People in this corner of the grid may spend all day rehearsing over and over the terrible things that have happened to them. They may even cry bitterly over their dilemma. But they tell the same story for years. As you turn off in your awareness what they are complaining about, you may even wonder if you've become calloused to their pain—until you realize that their "pain" has become a way of life, a way to avoid living. They love to talk about their problem, but solving the problem is everyone else's task, never theirs.

Emotional deadness may also be experienced as you have lunch with someone and find that you are suddenly quite sleepy. You're not tired, but as you listen to your friend you keep trying to stifle a yawn and struggle to stay awake. As you leave your luncheon, and leave your emotionally dead friend, you find you are no longer sleepy. Your sleepy reaction was a reaction to your friend's emotional deadness. Your friend's choice is one of hopelessness and increasing despair.

But there is a fourth option—the path of growth in the direction of self-control. This option is open to everyone. Just because your score on the questionnaire shows you as either a Spontaneous/

Flexible person or as a Decisive/Orderly person, you are not doomed to a lifetime of being overwhelmed by or overcontrolling of your emotions and feelings. Your score only indicates your area of comfort, or the general tendency of your personality and temperament. The potential for growth is available to anyone willing to develop the self-discipline and the ability to celebrate life that lead to self-control.

The rest of this book is about the key that can unlock the gate to that exciting, life-changing pathway of *growth*. And the process revolves around an exciting concept: Self-Talk.

Questions for Personal Growth and Discussion

1. In what area of your life would you like to experience more self-control?

2. What are some of the good features about your coping style? What are some of the negative features?

3. Where are you on the grid? Describe some of your feelings and actions when you are either overwhelmed by or overcontrolling of your emotions.

TWO

I Am What I Think

Men are disturbed, not by things, but by the view they take of them.

Epictetus

In the last chapter we met four people who felt out of control. They each had different ways of coping with the pressures of life, but they had in common the feeling of helplessness—of not being able to properly arrange the circumstances of their lives.

If you could talk with them about why they act or feel the way they do, they might suggest that if things had just been different in their lives, they would have been able to get a handle on their emotions. They would say they are the way they are and act the way they do because of forces in their lives that made them that way.

Most of us relate the cause of how we feel to the events in our lives. If good things happen to us, we feel happy and satisfied. If bad things happen to us, we feel sad or mad. As a result, we spend all kinds of effort trying to rearrange the circumstances of our lives in order to ensure our happiness.

We are bothered by examples that contradict that idea, such as people who are worse off than we are yet appear to be happy and content with life. Or when everything seems to be OK—there is money in the bank, the bills are paid, the kids are behaving, and our spouse is attentive—yet we have an underlying sense of doom and gloom that's totally unrelated to anything going on in our life. Perhaps we try to dismiss those depressing feelings by saying, "Well, that's me. I'm just a pessimist!" Or we look at those happy, contented people living in the midst of stress and turmoil and dismiss the apparent conflict by saying, "Well, I guess they're just naive optimists."

But our attempts to rationalize these contradictory situations aren't convincing. We have been taught to believe that our feelings and emotions are determined by the events in our lives. Our culture, through the media—especially the advertising media—continually reinforces this belief. Are you unhappy? Then try this new mouthwash! Feeling lonely because no one will talk to you? Then try our shampoo and get rid of that offensive dandruff. Can't sleep? Try our new remedy in a capsule. The examples go on and on.

The truth is that our emotions and behavior are *not* dependent on what is going on around us in our environment. We can change mouthwashes and still be unhappy. We can use the new shampoo and still feel lonely. We can take a pill and still lie there wide awake. The reason is that something else is at work that determines emotional and behavioral responses to life situations. The cognitive theorists suggest that this additional factor is our thoughts, or belief systems. These thoughts, or belief systems, are what I call Self-Talk.

The ABCs of Our Emotions

What we have been referring to as our circumstances—good or bad—is that outside world we were talking about in the first chapter. Ellis, in describing the ABCs of our emotions, calls this environment or circumstances *A*, or the *activating events* in our lives. This includes everything going on in our world. The natural tendency for people in our culture is to blame these activating events for causing us to act and feel the way we do. Ellis calls these emotional and behavioral *consequences* the *C*.

$$A = C$$

For example, someone doesn't return my phone call, and soon I feel hurt and rejected. That's like saying:

A (failure to return my phone call) = *C* (I feel hurt and rejected)

Other examples could include:

I got a *D* on my test = I'm stupid and dumb
Sally didn't invite me = I'm ugly and lonely
I didn't get a raise = I'm going to lose my job
The kids are fighting = I'm angry
She won't stop yelling at me = She makes me so angry!

You could write countless other examples into the parentheses:

$$A (\quad) = C (\quad)$$
$$A (\quad) = C (\quad)$$
$$A (\quad) = C (\quad)$$

However, when we accept the formula that *A* = *C*, we are ignoring our ABCs! If we know our alphabet, we can see that a *B* comes between the *A* and the *C*; and the *B* refers to our belief systems. These belief systems are our thought patterns—our Self-Talk. And these thoughts, which may not always be obvious to us, are the causes of our emotional and behavioral responses. Look at the example of someone's failure to return my phone call:

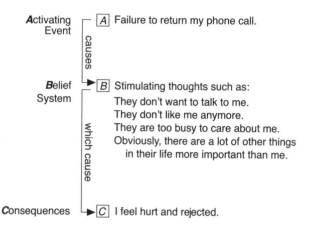

So our formula reads this way:

$$A + B = C$$

Self-Talk

Self-Talk refers to our belief systems or patterns of thoughts—the *B* in the formula. These belief systems can take the form of either private speech, thoughts, or external speech (the words we speak with our mouths). We usually speak out loud at the rate of 150 to 200 words per minute. Some research suggests that we talk privately to ourselves in our thoughts at the rate of approximately 1300 words per minute. That's a lot of talking!

Other studies suggest that since many of our thoughts take the form of mental images or concepts, we can think of something in a fleeting moment that would take us many minutes of verbal speech to describe. Even one word in our thoughts can be so saturated with meaning that hundreds of verbal words would be required to explain it. Self-Talk is a powerful force that is already at work within our lives. We need only to learn how to use this force for positive change.

Five basic principles form the foundation for Self-Talk.

1. *Our Thoughts Create Our Emotions*

It is quickly obvious that Self-Talk is anything but new. Epictetus, a Greek philosopher of the first century, was recorded in the *Enchiridion* as saying that "men are disturbed, not by things, but by the view they take of them." He understood that in every situation, our responses are based on how we choose to interpret that event. And that choice creates our emotions.

What Epictetus thought he discovered goes back even further. Proverbs 23:7 tells us that "as he thinketh in his heart, so is he." And Jeremiah gives us a written record that clearly illustrates this principle. In Lamentations 3 Jeremiah is depressed. That's really putting it mildly—if he wrote this today he would probably be hospitalized. Notice the symptoms:

> I am the man who has seen affliction
> under the rod of his [God's] wrath;
> he has driven and brought me
> into darkness without any light;
> surely against me he turns his hand
> again and again the whole day long.
> verses 1–3

What misery and hopelessness! God is oppressing Jeremiah, he believes, making him suffer this horrible emotional distress. But it gets worse. Jeremiah has physical symptoms as well.

> He [God] has made my flesh and my skin waste away,
> and broken my bones.
> verse 4

His body aches! When people are deeply depressed, their bones ache, and their bodies begin to feel as if they are wasting away from lack of food. Perhaps, at this point, Jeremiah's depression is making him physically ill. And that only adds to his feelings of bitterness and anguish.

> He has besieged and enveloped me
>> with bitterness and tribulation;
> he has made me dwell in darkness
>> like the dead of long ago.
>>>> verses 5–6

Jeremiah is now describing a terrible feeling of being trapped—a very modern feeling.

> He has walled me about so that I cannot escape;
>> he has put heavy chains on me;
> though I call and cry for help,
>> he shuts out my prayer;
> he has blocked my ways with hewn stones,
>> he has made my paths crooked.
>>>> verses 7–9

Remember, Jeremiah is blaming God for all these feelings: God is shutting out his prayer. God is blocking his way. God is setting up the trap for him. It is God's fault that Jeremiah feels so trapped, so hopeless, so out of control.

But now Jeremiah adds another symptom. He's afraid. He thinks God is out to get him, and he can trust no one. Even his friends are out to get him.

> He is to me like a bear lying in wait,
>> like a lion in hiding;
> he led me off my way and tore me to pieces;
>> he has made me desolate;
> he bent his bow and set me
>> as a mark for his arrow.

> He drove into my heart
>> the arrows of his quiver;
> I have become the laughingstock of all peoples,
>> the burden of their songs all day long.
> He has filled me with bitterness,
>> he has sated me with wormwood.
>
> verses 10–15

Again, Jeremiah comes back to the physical distress that is coupled with his total feeling of despair.

> He has made my teeth grind on gravel,
>> and made me cower in ashes;
> my soul is bereft of peace,
>> I have forgotten what happiness is.
>
> verses 16–17

Of course he has! His happiness is gone. What else would one expect when the circumstances of his life (the A) are so miserable!

> So I say, "Gone is my glory,
>> and my expectation from the LORD."
>
> verse 18

Now he wants to grovel in his misery. So he gives himself permission to wallow in all those preceding thoughts.

> Remember my affliction and my bitterness,
>> the wormwood and the gall!
> My soul continually thinks of it
>> and is bowed down within me.
>
> verses 19–20

Here's the key! Jeremiah *continually thinks* of his misery. No wonder he's depressed. It's not all the awful events in his life that are causing his grief; it's his choice of thoughts about these events, his Self-Talk, that determines what he is feeling. But now Jeremiah begins to change. Perhaps he becomes aware of his choice to continue to grovel in bitterness. And that awareness allows him to reverse the pattern of his thoughts. Verse 21 says:

> But this I call to mind,
> and therefore I have hope.

Now note what follows that change in Jeremiah's Self-Talk. With his choice to focus on a ray of hope, his emotions change.

> The steadfast love of the LORD never ceases,
> his mercies never come to an end;
> they are new every morning;
> great is thy faithfulness.
> "The LORD is my portion," says my soul,
> "therefore I will hope in him."
>
> verses 22–24

Jeremiah moves from the pit of total despair to the soaring mountaintops of faith and exultation! And he does this with his thoughts. In verse 18 he said, "Gone is my glory, and my expectation from the LORD." What a depressing, hopeless thought! But in verse 24 he says, "The LORD is my portion, therefore I will hope in him." In verse 18 Jeremiah thinks about his misery and he feels hopeless; in verse 24 he thinks about the faithfulness of God and he feels hope! His thoughts create his emotions. He regains self-control through Self-Talk.

You can test this principle yourself. When you finish reading this paragraph, put the book down and close your eyes. With your eyes closed, take a few slow, deep breaths to help you relax, and then take one minute and make yourself feel sad. Have someone tell you when the minute is up. Then take another minute and make yourself feel happy. Then open your eyes.

Now, how did you do that? When I do this with audiences, I always ask them how they did it. And I always get one of two answers. Either the person thought about some sad experience to feel sadness and thought about some happy experience to feel happy, or he or she visually imagined some sad or happy experience.

Obviously, nothing changed in your external world during those two minutes to make you feel happy or sad, just as nothing happened in Jeremiah's external world between verse 18 and verse 24. But your emotions changed! And they changed because of your Self-Talk.

This is the basic point of the ABCs of your emotions. The emotional consequences of any activating event are not created by that event. *C* is not caused by *A*! It is created by your belief systems—Self-Talk—which is the *B* surrounding that event.

It is Self-Talk that explains why someone can experience inner rest and peace in the midst of the most wrenching experiences of life. It is also the reason a person can ignore all the positive, pleasant events occurring in his or her life and focus on a worry and become miserable. Thoughts create emotions!

2. Our Thoughts Affect Our Behavior

An oft-told story illustrates this point. Some years ago a man was traveling across the country by sneaking rides on freight trains. One particular night he climbed into what looked like a boxcar and closed the door. Somehow the door locked shut, and he was trapped inside. When his eyes became adjusted to the darkness, he found that he was inside a refrigerated boxcar. He was freezing cold. All the noise he could make inside the car failed to attract anyone's attention. He hopelessly gave up and lay down on the floor of the railroad car.

As he tried to fight against the cold, he scratched part of a message on the floor of the car. He never finished. Some time late the next day, repairmen from the railroad opened the door of the refrigerated boxcar and found the man dead. He looked like someone who had frozen to death. The problem was that the refrigeration units on the car were not working. The repairmen had come to fix those units. The temperature inside the car probably did not go below fifty degrees during the night. The man died because his thoughts told him he was freezing to death!

If our emotions are determined by our thoughts, it follows that our thoughts will also strongly affect our behavior. In the examples in the first chapter, each person's thoughts about losing control or of being unable to maintain self-control appeared to be the motivating force behind his or her behavior. Donna's fainting spells were all related to fear, and her fear was an emotion created by her thoughts. Marge's escape to the shopping mall was based on her thought patterns, which interpreted everything as being overwhelming. Peggy's driving, compulsive behavior was motivated by her belief that she had to demand perfection of herself and everyone else. Arnie's refusal to talk about his son was the result of choices he made to exclude certain painful experiences from his awareness.

This may appear to be an oversimplification. But the consistent principle is that all of them behaved as they did because of their belief systems—their Self-Talk.

Shyness is another example. Almost everyone has experienced shyness at some time in life. For many, though, it is an ongoing experience. But shyness is based on a belief system. You behave as a shy person because your behavior is controlled by the belief that you're shy. Try it. The next time you experience shyness, listen to your Self-Talk. The core statement in your thoughts is "I can't do that because I'm shy." Our Self-Talk, working through our emotions, is a major determiner of our behavior.

3. Our Perceived Center of Control Affects Our Behavior

It is not what is occurring in our lives that affects our behavior; it is what we *believe* about what is occurring that matters. If we focus on the facts related to an out-of-control world, we will behave in a certain manner. If we focus on a world under the control of an all-powerful God, we will behave in a different way.

The twelve men sent by Moses to spy out the land provide a good illustration of this principle. The spies all saw the same people and the same land. For forty days they checked out everything about the land flowing with milk and honey. Then they returned to Moses with a report. In Numbers 13 we see that Joshua and Caleb came back excited. They were ready to move forward. Caleb said, "Let us go up at once, and occupy it; for we are well able to overcome it" (v. 30).

But the other ten men disagreed. Apparently, on the way back to the camp where Moses and the people waited, they started to think about the battles they would need to fight. As they walked along, the Nephilim (the giants of the land) started looking taller. Their thoughts began to turn these tall men into fierce monsters, and at the same time they saw themselves beginning to shrink.

Finally, as they stood before the people, the land that flowed with milk and honey had changed into "a land that devours its inhabitants; and *all* the people that we saw in it are men of great stature. And there we saw the Nephilim (the sons of Anak, who come from the Nephilim); and *we seemed to ourselves like grasshoppers,* and so we seemed to them" (Num. 13:32–33, italics added). That was their *perception* of the situation.

These men developed a "grasshopper complex." Their thoughts exaggerated the size of all the men of the land in the same way their Self-Talk exaggerated their own weaknesses. During those forty days, they shifted the focus of their attention away from the all-powerful God, who had only recently demonstrated his power by making a way for them to cross the Red Sea and then destroying the pursuing Egyptian army.

Joshua and Caleb did not allow their Self-Talk to pull them into that trap. They kept God as their center of control. They looked at the same tall men and said, with God, "We are able to overcome!" The other ten spies looked at the tall men and said, "We are grasshoppers!" They saw the same thing. But their behavior was determined by what or who they thought was in control of the situation. Even though their eyes saw the same land and people that Joshua and Caleb saw, their perceptions differed. And their perceptions of the tall men and the land shaped their belief systems—their Self-Talk.

4. We Think Irrationally

Now we can begin to understand why we are so easily caught in an out-of-control cycle, becoming either overwhelmed or overcontrolling. We can also see how easy it was for the people of Israel to believe the ten men and to reject the report of Joshua and Caleb. We all tend to think irrationally.

All of us can remember situations in which we acted in a certain way that embarrassed us. We were embarrassed because later we could see just how irrational our ideas were at the time. So often we do this with those we love the most. We become angry with our spouse and say things we don't mean. Those cruel statements haunt us later, as we feel guilty for hurting the one we love.

Or we get caught in this trap with our children. We worry about them. And our worries escalate to the point where we just must confront them. Perhaps we go so far as to accuse our kids of doing what we fear they *might* do; and then they react with anger and hurt. Later on, after everyone cools off, we berate ourselves for saying such dumb things. We say these things because we think irrationally.

Perhaps a clear example is one of a beautiful girl who thinks she's ugly. Every time someone compliments her on her looks, she protests about how terrible she looks. And the more someone tries to affirm the compliment, the more she paints herself as ugly and plain. Nothing can convince her, because she thinks irrationally.

One of the best illustrations of irrational thinking is in the account of Job. I've always struggled with the character of Job. Everything that happens to him seems so unfair! But recently I've come to see Job in a different light.

Job has everything a man can hope for. He has enough wealth that he can spend his time as he pleases. His children are on their own and his business runs itself quite efficiently. But Job is a worrier! In the first chapter we meet him as he offers burnt offerings for each of his children, for Job says, "It may be that my sons have sinned, and cursed God in their hearts." Then verse 5 adds, "Thus Job did continually"! His behavior is compulsive.

"What if . . ." could be Job's motto. As a result he becomes meticulous in his worship and in his life. And this leads to the problems he encounters. In the midst of his lament, we discover a clue as to why these terrible things happened to him. He asks:

> Why is light given to him that is in misery,
> and life to the bitter in soul,
> who long for death, but it comes not,
> and dig for it more than for hid treasures;
> who rejoice exceedingly,
> and are glad, when they find the grave?

Why is light given to a man whose way is hid,
  whom God has hedged in?
For my sighing comes as my bread,
  and my groanings are poured out like water.
For the thing that I fear comes upon me,
  and what I dread befalls me.
I am not at ease, nor am I quiet;
  I have no rest; but trouble comes.

Job 3:20–26, italics added

Quite clearly, Job has reason to grieve and to long for the end of his life. His pain and sufferings are deep. But note verse 25: "For the thing that I fear comes upon me, and what I dread befalls me." We've already seen that Job is a worrier, but we didn't know just how much he worries. We can almost picture him as he walks to the town square to spend the day talking with the other wise men. He walks slowly and worries much. He worries about the sheep. Were any stolen? Are his servants being honest with him? He worries about the weather and the effect it will have on his crops. He worries about his children and his wife. He probably even worries about himself, whether or not he has covered every possible sin with his last sacrifice. Perhaps he even worries about his sacrifices, whether the animal offered is really the best one, or if he had spent a little more time, he could have found a better one. His mind is constantly preoccupied with worry.

From all outward appearances, Job has absolutely nothing to worry about. He has everything he needs. But he worries about everything! And by the third chapter, the things Job worries about become a reality.

Imagine the scene in heaven as described in the opening chapters of the book. Satan goes to God, and God comments on his servant Job. Job is a man who fears God, and God points that out.

But Satan reminds God of the hedge he has built around Job. But the hedge isn't there! His protection is gone!

Job has been busy trimming the hedge with his worries. Each day he has gone out and tried to make the hedge a little straighter, a little neater. But he has never been satisfied with his work. And he has trimmed until the hedge is gone! His worried Self-Talk has trimmed the hedge, giving Satan an opportunity to attack. Job's Self-Talk is irrational!

We've built ourselves a discouraging spiral. If our thoughts create our emotions, and if our thoughts affect our behavior, and if it is our perceived center of control that also affects our behavior, and if we all tend to think irrationally, what chance do we have to regain control of ourselves and our emotions? How can we break the cycle?

5. We Create Change in Our Lives by Gaining Control of Our Thoughts

There is hope! The cycle can be broken! We can experience self-control. And the battleground is in our minds. If our thoughts are creating our emotions, we can change our emotions by changing our thoughts. That's what Jeremiah did. That is also what we can do!

We still have a choice in determining how we will feel and act. The apostle Paul understood this. In several places he reminds us that the hard work of self-control begins in our minds. In 2 Corinthians 10:3–5, he shows us that the battle is not taking place in the physical, external environment; rather, it is in our minds. We are to "destroy arguments and every proud obstacle to the knowledge of God, and take every thought captive to obey Christ." We are literally to fight against the arguments and irrational reasonings of our minds. We are to capture these thoughts, change them, and bring them into obedience to Christ.

How do we do that? Paul answers that question for us in Philippians 4:8. Every thought that enters our mind is to be about whatever is true, honorable, just, pure, lovely, or gracious. "If there is any excellence, if there is anything worthy of praise, think about these things." And the promise is that "the God of peace will be with you" (v. 9).

Guard your mind! Watch what you think! Don't allow *anything* that doesn't measure up to this criteria to enter your mind or find a place to settle. You experience self-control by controlling your thinking. And you do that by capturing every thought that enters your mind and examining it to see if it is worthy of finding a place in your belief systems. If it fails the test, you argue with it, debate and dispute with its irrationality, and then get rid of it quickly.

In Romans 12:2 Paul continues with this idea. First he warns us to "not be conformed to this world," or as J. B. Phillips translates it, "Don't let the world around you squeeze you into its own mold." Don't get caught in the trap of irrational thinking. Don't accept the false idea that your emotions, feelings, and behavior are controlled by the events in your life. Reject that principle!

Instead, Paul tells you to "be transformed by the renewal of your mind"! He says you can be changed. And the key to transformation is in the renewing of your mind! Change your thoughts—your Self-Talk—and you change your life!

Questions for Personal Growth and Discussion

1. What did you think today that caused you to feel a certain way?

2. Think of some of the things you said or thought this week that were examples of irrational belief systems. What made them irrational?

3. What changes could you make in your Self-Talk that would cause positive changes in your behavior this week?

THREE

Self-Talk

Words of Faith

> Faith is . . . the evidence of things not seen.
>
> Hebrews 11:1 KJV

Words, said either in the privacy of the mind or spoken aloud, are powerful. Written across the pages of history are phrases uttered at crucial moments that turned the course of world events. At the beginning of World War II, Winston Churchill told the British people that even though all of Europe might fall, "We shall not flag or fail. We shall go on to the end . . . we shall fight on the seas and oceans . . . we shall fight on the beaches, we shall fight on the landing grounds, we shall fight in the fields and in the streets, we shall fight in the hills; we shall never surrender." And the free world rallied to the task.

Franklin D. Roosevelt told a nation broken by the Great Depression that "the only thing we have to fear is fear itself." And people responded with courage. John Paul Jones responded to the British demand that his ship surrender with the words, "I have not yet begun to fight." And not only did his men fight courageously, but his words have inspired naval men down through the centuries.

Abraham Lincoln scrawled a short speech on an envelope and delivered his Gettysburg Address. His words touched the heart of a nation and started the process of healing the wounds caused by the Civil War.

The list goes on and on. Look back through the pages of the Old Testament. David, as a young man, affirms his faith to King Saul and then to the giant Goliath. He tells the king, "The LORD who delivered me from the paw of the lion and from the paw of the bear, will deliver me from the hand of this Philistine" (1 Sam. 17:37). Then, as David goes out to meet the giant, Goliath curses him. And David responds with powerful words: "I come to you in the name of the LORD of hosts, the God of the armies of Israel, whom you have defied. This day the LORD will deliver you into my hand" (vv. 45–46). And history records the results.

Now that is not to say that the words, in and of themselves, are miracle workers. They are the reflections of what is in the heart and mind of David. And they release within David's life the power of God. They are an extension of his Self-Talk during the years prior to that event. They are an expression of his faith.

Words Release Faith

Most of us think of faith as being trust in some positive, benevolent deity. But faith is a process of life. No one is faith*less*. It is not a question of whether we possess faith or not. It is rather a question of where we place our faith. And our thoughts are the best barometers of the object of our faith. Faith is a process that works in releasing life-changing power in either a positive or negative direction.

For example, have you ever noticed how much more tired you feel after yawning and saying, "I'm so tired"? You feel more tired because your Self-Talk has just released power in the direction of tiredness.

In the same way, recent studies have shown that people who begin to talk about the possibility of divorce often find themselves proceeding inevitably in the direction of divorce. Later they comment on how they felt trapped by their words. Things were not that bad, but talking about divorce gave power to that possibility.

I spoke recently with a successful businessman. He had started a new business and worked hard. The result of his work was solid growth, a good management team, and unlimited potential in the years ahead. But increasingly, the demands of the business claimed more and more of his time. Then he passed out as he was leading an important meeting. The doctors told him he had to stop all activity for three months and then limit himself carefully for the next six months. As we talked he commented, "Dave, I've been saying for a year that nothing can stop me, except getting sick." He determined by his statement that the only way he could slow down was to get sick. He had set himself up! And every time he thought or said those words, he released faith in that statement. And what he believed came true.

In the Gospel of Matthew there is an interesting contrast made regarding three miracles. In chapter 8 a centurion comes to Jesus and tells him about his servant, who is paralyzed and in terrible distress. Jesus offers to go and heal the servant, but the centurion says, "Lord, I am not worthy to have you come under my roof; but only say the word, and my servant will be healed" (v. 8). Jesus marvels at the man's faith and says, "Go; be it done for you as you have believed" (v. 13). And the servant is healed.

In chapter 9 a ruler comes to Jesus and says, "My daughter has just died; but come and lay your hand on her, and she will live" (v. 18). Later in the chapter we read that Jesus goes to the house, puts his hand on her hand, and she lives. While going to the ruler's house, he is interrupted by a woman who has been bleeding for twelve years. The woman says to herself (using Self-Talk), "If I only touch his garment, I shall be made well" (v. 21). And as she touches his garment, power flows out of Jesus and she becomes well.

Three miracles, each taking place in a different way. In each one, Jesus could have said what he said to the centurion, "Be it done for you as you have believed." What they believe, what they say in their thoughts or with their mouth, determines how Jesus performs the miracle. The centurion says, "Don't bother coming to my house, just say the word." The ruler says, "Come and put your hand on her." And the woman tells herself, "I must touch his garment." And what they believe is what they see take place! Great power is released by our thoughts and our words.

The book of Proverbs expands on this theme. Proverbs 6:2 points out that we can be "snared in the utterance of [our] lips, caught in the words of [our] mouth." Therefore, be careful what you say. Solomon writes in Proverbs 10:24, "What the wicked dreads will come upon him, but the desire of the righteous will be granted." Be careful, he is saying, because what we think and say have a way of coming true.

In Proverbs 13:3 this warning is added: "He who guards his mouth preserves his life; he who opens wide his lips comes to ruin." This theme is picked up again in Proverbs 18:21, where we read, "Death and life are in the power of the tongue." The writer is saying that in our words and thoughts we have the ability to speak life to ourselves in the same way that we can speak death to ourselves. With the growing acceptance of the fact that between 75 and 90 percent of all illnesses are caused by the body's response to stress, these two proverbs have added significance. When we allow the life-draining emotions of lingering anger, guilt, anxiety, and fear to be the controlling forces of our emotions, we are giving death and disease power in our life!

Perhaps that is why David practices positive Self-Talk, as in Psalm 103. I'm not sure what stress points are being stretched in his life, but he retains self-control by guarding carefully his thoughts. He tells himself to bless the Lord. And after repeating that command several times to his mind, he then lists a number of reasons why he can bless the Lord. He begins by telling himself,

> Bless the Lord, O my soul;
>> and all that is within me, bless his holy name!
> Bless the Lord, O my soul,
>> and forget not all his benefits.

He becomes so excited in the process that he ends the psalm by saying to himself and everyone else,

> Bless the Lord, O you his angels,
>> you mighty ones who do his word,
>> hearkening to the voice of his word!
> Bless the Lord, all his hosts,
>> his ministers that do his will!
> Bless the Lord, all his works,
>> in all places of his dominion.
> Bless the Lord, O my soul!

These principles are universal. They work not only for those whose lives are recorded on the pages of the Bible, they work in our lives as well. Think you're getting a cold? Watch out, you've got it! Think you're getting a headache? It's yours. Think you're going to have a rough day at work? You own it! Think your kids are going to act up at Grandma's house? Never fails.

The Power of Words and Images

Some years back a man I knew watched his mother die of cancer. On the way home from the cemetery, he said to his wife, "I'll probably die of cancer too." From that point on he was convinced he had cancer. At first, doctors assured him there was no sign of the feared disease. But he was still convinced that soon he would be dead of cancer. And soon the doctors did find a tumor. Within a year of his mother's death, he died of cancer.

At the time it happened, I didn't think too much about the connection between his words and his death. I do remember that I wasn't comfortable with what I had witnessed. I thought of it again some years later when I first read of a doctor's research with people diagnosed as having terminal cancer, meaning they had less than a year to live. Along with the medical treatment this physician supervised, he asked his patients to spend time daily creating visual images in their minds. In these images, the patients were to see the cancer cells as some evil invading force. They were also told to see the white blood cells in their bodies becoming a very aggressive force, attacking and defeating the evil cancer cells. When the battle was finished, other white blood cells would come along and clean up the battleground.

Sometimes the white cells became white knights, riding on magnificent stallions as they met and defeated the invading hordes of evil. Others saw the white cells as white cats, clearing the neighborhood of dirty, evil mice. It didn't matter how the images were formed, as long as the white blood cells were the victors. The results he reported were miraculous.

In his book, *Getting Well Again,* Dr. Simonton and his wife update the results of his research. The recent findings are even more amazing. Not only have people experienced complete remission from terminal cancer but some have also used the same process to experience complete remission of arthritis, asthma, and other painful diseases. People who were expected to live less than a year have not only outlived the prognosis by at least twice that, they have also lived a more active, normal life. The difference between the treatment used by Dr. Simonton and that used by other medical treatment centers is that Dr. Simonton's staff tapped into the power of the mind—of Self-Talk!

Dr. David Bressler, head of the UCLA pain clinic, works with people suffering from chronic pain. These people experience constant suffering, some the result of injuries and others the result of causes not known. One of the successful forms of therapy involves the use of visual images in the mind. In this process of mental imagery, Dr. Bressler sometimes has the patients visualize what the pain looks like. Once they have a visual image of the pain in mind, they work on changing the image of the pain, reducing its size and intensity. In the process the actual pain is also reduced in size and intensity.

In my own counseling practice, I have worked with many people with weight problems. One of the most important parts of the treatment is for the individuals to regularly practice creating a visual image of themselves as thin. The degree of difficulty in ridding the body of excess weight is related to the difficulty they have creating that mental image of themselves fifty or one hundred pounds thinner.

The mind is incredible. No wonder David wrote,

You made all the delicate, inner parts of my body, and knit them together in my mother's womb. Thank you for making me so wonderfully complex! It is amazing to think about. Your workmanship is marvelous.

Psalm 139:13–14 TLB

One of the most interesting applications of Self-Talk is in work with hyperactive, impulsive children. In Dr. Donald Meichenbaum's work, he would first model for the child the task that needed to be done. While performing the task, the adult talks out loud to himself, telling himself what to do. Then the child is asked to attempt to perform the same task while instructing himself aloud, just as the adult has done. Gradually, the verbal instructions given to himself will be whispered and then internalized into private speech or thoughts. A variety of tasks are used, from the simple task of drawing a line to the complex task of learning to drive a car. In some of his later work, Meichenbaum has children not only give themselves instructions both verbally and internally but also begin to use visual images in the mind. In these mental images, these hyperactive children are to practice seeing themselves performing a specific task more slowly. Sometimes the mental image is simple. For example, they are to visualize themselves walking instead of running. In the process, the children build new belief systems that help them to learn how to effectively control their behavior.

The same type of experiment was done with patients in a mental institution. Schizophrenics were taught a set of self-controlling self-statements. These statements not only helped these patients with self-care, such as feeding themselves, but also gave them a way to modify their perception of themselves and their symptoms.

In both types of cases, the research indicated that neither the hyperactive, impulsive children nor the schizophrenic patients had previously been able to develop the internalization of language.

Without organized Self-Talk, they had no effective way to deal with the world. As a result, they became problems to their families and to society. Proper Self-Talk was the missing ingredient.

All of these examples illustrate the importance of our Self-Talk. We all talk to ourselves, sometimes out loud, but most of the time in the privacy of our minds. The result is always the same—the things we say determine the way we live our lives.

What are you in the habit of saying? What kinds of expressions would your family or friends recognize as being typical of you? You may have simply passed off some of these remarks as not being serious or even as jokes. But what you say and think is a very important indicator of where you are placing your faith.

Take some time now, before reading the next chapter, to make a list of the kinds of Self-Talk you usually make. What kinds of things do you say out loud? What kinds of statements do you make about yourself in your thoughts? For example, do you say or think things like:

I can't do this job; it's too hard.

I'm always late. Guess I'll be late for my wedding, even.

I'm so shy, I couldn't talk to him.

Write down some of the statements you make, in the space below:

Now make another list, writing down some of the statements you want to begin to make about yourself. For example, you could change the above statements to read:

I don't like this job, but step-by-step I can do it.

I've had a habit of being late, but I can change my schedule and be on time.

I feel nervous about talking to him, but I'm going to.

Write down some of your new Self-Talk statements:

Questions for Personal Growth and Discussion

1. In comparing the two lists you made, what differences do you experience in your feelings with each list? Explain.

2. How did the words you spoke this week affect what happened to you?

3. Look at the list you made of the expressions you usually say. In what does it appear you place your faith?

FOUR

What Shapes
Our Self-Talk?

Consider the quarry from which you were mined, the rock
from which you were cut! Yes, think about your ancestors.

Isaiah 51:1–2 TLB

Growing up is the most complex, demanding task any of us will
ever experience in our lifetime. As more research is done in the
area of child development, the list grows longer as to what children
need from the parental environment in order to become relatively
healthy adults.

Every parent does an imperfect job of parenting—that's a given
since we live in a sinful world full of imperfect, sinful people. And
each of us is affected by these imperfections. So if we want to understand why we struggle with the issues we do, we need to look to
our parents. It's probably related to some inadequacy in the way
they parented us, caused by their imperfections.

But why did they do what they did while raising us? Probably because of their own parents' inadequacies. And why did their parents do that? Because of their parents. We can go backwards in time asking the same why question until we finally get to Adam and Eve.

Suppose we confront Adam and ask him why he did what he did. He has no parent to turn to, so he turns to Eve, the only other human around, and says, "It was (because of) the woman you (God) gave me! She did it." When we turn and ask Eve why she did what she did, she has no other human to turn to, so she thinks quickly and says, "The serpent tricked me" (see Gen. 3:12–13). When we get back to the serpent, we get back to the source of the reality of sin, and then we get an accurate appraisal of the situation.

One can accurately say that the gaps, the places in our growth and development where there was something missing, are the result of being born into this race of sinful human beings—no one is exempt. But the gaps in my experience, either of actions taken or not taken during my growing up years, are my experiences, and that is what makes my struggles uniquely mine.

Things That Shape Our Self-Talk

Families are both fascinating and paradoxical. They are always changing, while at the same time they are always staying the same. That may sound like a contradiction, but it really is what happens. The changes we attempt to make in our families take place on one level. But these are usually superficial, for underneath these "changes" things don't really change. Let me illustrate. The family I experienced as I was growing up as the firstborn was quite different from the family my sister experienced as the second child and the youngest. When I was born, I had my parents' total attention.

There were only three of us in the family. When my sister was born, I was already there. She had to share our parents with me. Instead of three, now there were four. As I grew up, I always had in the background of my mind that sense of family as three, something my sister never experienced.

But underneath those different experiences of our family, things stayed pretty much the same. The gaps in my parents' ability to parent were the same for me as for my sister. My parents' ability to experience closeness, to discipline appropriately, to train us in godliness—all of these along with other tasks were equally limited in their relationship with both my sister and myself. And no matter what we did to try to make changes in the way our family worked, the lack of emotional closeness, the communication patterns, the avoidance of problems, the way decisions were made—all of these stayed the same. It's these underlying patterns that are usually more difficult to identify but that have the more powerful effect on the struggles we face as adults. These underlying, unchanging patterns feed us the messages that are the basis for our adult Self-Talk, both positive and negative.

Moreover, there are often events in the life of the family that bring to the forefront the inadequacies or limitations of parents. For example, the physical illness or physical disability of a family member, the abuse of alcohol or drugs by a parent or child, the emotional illness of a parent, the mental disability of one child, the sexual perversion or obsession by a parent, the death or suicide of one of the family members, the divorce of the parents and the subsequent remarriage and blending of families, or the struggles of the single-parent family. Any one of these adds stress to the family system and adds to the distortions we have in our beliefs about ourselves, about others, about the world, and about God.

Moreover, destructive generational patterns are present in some families, what the Bible refers to as the "sins of the fathers," which affect even the third and fourth generations (see Exod. 34:7). This shows us how neglect or abuse in past generations can play an important role in shaping our Self-Talk as adults.

No parents can control all the powerful forces that shape the lives of their children. If our parents did try to control them all, that effort in itself would have a different but profound impact and would probably give us an even less effective way of coping as adults.

To help us understand how our family of origin shaped our patterns of Self-Talk and our belief systems about life, let's look specifically at some of the general patterns of negative experiences we can have during our growing up years.

The Child Becomes as a Parent

Some of us grew up in homes where one or both parents was severely limited due to such things as alcoholism, workaholism, emotional neglect, or prolonged absence from the home. This creates a leadership vacuum in the family, which, quite often, one or more of the children will try to fill.

Becky was the oldest of eight children. For as long as she can remember, she has known that her mom went to several different doctors, all supposedly for the same problem. What she didn't know until she was an adult was that her mom had used these doctors to obtain large amounts of pain medication and tranquilizers. Mom was a drug addict—addicted to prescription drugs.

Becky's dad was a salesman. He was gone most of every week, coming home on weekends. When he did come home, his time and energy were spent fighting with Becky's mom. Neither parent gave any energy to being a parent. Into the leadership vacuum within that home stepped Becky. Up until the time Becky got married, she filled the role of mother to her mother and to her siblings. Because of this, she never had much time for the typical activities of children or high schoolers.

Becky married a man who traveled a lot in his work. Over the years she had six children, and now in her forties, she is exhausted. "I've been a mother for as long as I can remember. Isn't there something else to life?" she asked. As we talked, it was clear that her Self-Talk revolves around a number of distortions that excuse her husband from any involvement with the children and explain away any of her own needs as being "selfish." Her Self-Talk includes thoughts like:

If I let up, who will take care of everything?

I must be responsible—I can't be like my mother.

I can't trust my husband with the kids; he can't even remember their birthdays. How could he remember to take care of them?

It's my job to take care of everything at home. I must do my job, or else I'll be a failure and my kids will suffer.

My friends just don't understand. I've got to make it work.

Any attempts on the part of family or friends to persuade her to let up and take some time to enjoy life are met by Becky's own arguments against herself. All Becky knows how to be is a parent, for that is all she has been for as long as she can remember.

Boundary Violations

Boundaries define the physical and emotional space between people. They are what allow me to be me and you to be you. One of our boundaries is our skin, which clearly defines our physical selves. We learn first about boundaries within our families, and it is there that we are supposed to learn what it means to be an individual—to be separate and different from everyone else in the family and therefore to be separate and different from everyone else in the world.

In some families, the boundaries between members are rigid. Little is shared between people in the family, and almost nothing is shared with people outside the family. As adults, people from this type of family find it very difficult to let anyone get close to them. Sometimes, in the early phase of a relationship, they feel close to another person. But that feeling quickly changes to fear. The fear can be that of being rejected, abandoned, or controlled. The closeness quickly disappears as fear begins to dominate their lives.

Other families have fuzzy boundaries. Parents intrude into the lives of their children, and individuality is not honored between siblings. Everything belongs to everyone, which results in nothing really belonging to anyone. As adults, people from this type of family often struggle with issues of independence and autonomy, feeling more comfortable in dependent relationships that don't allow for much individuality. Sometimes they believe that others can read their minds or know their hidden motives better than they do themselves. They don't have a lot of confidence in speaking their own minds.

Both of these boundary issues, either having fuzzy boundaries or rigid boundaries, deeply affect our understanding and beliefs about everything in our lives—our perception of ourselves, of others, of the world, and even of God. These boundary patterns are often seen consistently over several generations and are difficult to change. Many times in these families it seems like a lot is changing, but the changes are only superficial—underneath, everything stays the same.

In families with either kind of boundary problem the parents may directly victimize the children or they may fail to protect the children from being abused by others in some way. Because children from these families are not clear about boundaries between themselves and others, as they grow up they may even expose themselves to added hurt or exploitation in their attempts to build relationships.

Other examples of boundary issues that directly affect our Self-Talk include physical or sexual abuse, persistent violation of children's privacy, parents individually or together confiding in children things that are meant only for the parents, and other behaviors that confuse the natural boundaries between generations.

Current patterns in our Self-Talk that center on issues of shame and unworthiness are often based on boundary violations we experienced during our growing up years. These violations will feed our distorted belief systems, but that's not all. Studies show that if we grow up in families with boundary problems, we will experience with increased intensity a number of anxiety-based physical symptoms. These physical symptoms can show up in childhood but are more likely to show up in our adulthood.

Chronic Rejection

An experience of feeling rejected is one of the most expensive sources of our Self-Talk. When there is an experience of chronic rejection, the devastation and effects are profound and deep. Our Self-Talk will reflect that rejection and be filled with shameful feelings about ourselves.

We know that abused children crave attention so much that they will take the abuse because they are at least getting some kind of attention from the parent. But it is the kind of attention that is based on rejection. No matter how you look back at experiences of abuse, it will always end up as rejection.

But there are other reasons why some children grow up with a sense of chronic rejection. For example, in some families, sons are devalued and ignored and daughters are revered and put on a pedestal. In other families it's the daughters who are rejected and the sons who can do no wrong. Sometimes rejection and favoritism are part of the generational patterns within the family. We see this in the biblical patriarch Abraham's family.

When Abraham's son Ishmael was born, he was considered to be Sarah's son even though he was physically born to her slave Hagar. Finally, after all those years of barrenness, Sarah had the son she had longed for and been promised.

At first it didn't matter that the birth mother, Hagar, was always there. After all, she was Sarah's slave, and as a slave she couldn't even lay claim to her own child. And when neighbors of Abraham and Sarah came to visit, they didn't ask, "How's Hagar's boy?" They asked, "Sarah, let me see *your* son."

For fifteen years Abraham and Sarah enjoyed their son. But then some messengers from the Lord God came and told Abraham that having a son by Hagar wasn't what God had promised—Sarah would bear a son of her own! And nine months later when Isaac was born, a generational pattern of favoritism and rejection was set in motion.

It didn't take long for Sarah to switch her love and loyalty to her "real" son, Isaac. Soon after Isaac was weaned, Sarah looked at Ishmael and told Abraham to send him and his mother away! The matter distressed Abraham greatly because it was his son (see Gen. 21:11). For Abraham, both Ishmael and Isaac were equally his sons. It was not easy for him to send Ishmael away. But he did. So in this first generation of Abraham's family, one son was rejected and the other favored, and the result was that one son was sent away.

Years later, when Isaac prepared for marriage, I can't help but wonder if one of the things he said to himself was, "When I have children, it's going to be different. There'll be no favoritism in my family!" He knew his older brother, for when Abraham died, they both buried him. As a younger brother, he probably missed Ishmael after he was sent away. And so Isaac vowed to do it differently. I remember saying something like that when my first son was born— "I'm going to do it differently than my father. I'm going to spend time getting to know my son."

One of the patterns of Self-Talk many of us can identify with is this "I'm going to do it differently" pattern. But over time we realize how easy it is to speak about change and how nearly impossible it is to actually do it. We may do some things differently on the surface, but the resistance to changing the underlying patterns is so strong that we end up doing the things we so desperately wanted to avoid.

Isaac's family was different on the surface. He had two sons, like his father Abraham, but this time they were twin sons. And from the beginning, the whole family was divided down the middle. Rebekah loved Jacob; after all, he was a cute, delightful baby who God said would eventually rule over his older brother. Isaac enjoyed Esau, especially as the young man grew up enjoying "manly" things such as hunting and fishing.

In Isaac's family, even though he vowed he would do it differently, rejection still became the issue. Now one parent rejected one child, and the child rejected by that parent was accepted by the other parent. The rejection pattern was done differently, but the result was the same.

Look at the chain of events and its consequences. After Jacob deceived his elderly father and stole the blessing from his older brother, Esau was raging mad. In his anger he planned to kill Jacob. There was only one thing to do—send Jacob away. He must leave, for his mother didn't want to grieve over two men. So for the second generation in a row, one son was sent away. But look at how the intensity of the problem had increased. In the first generation, Ishmael was sent away because of Sarah's jealousy. In the second generation, Jacob was sent away out of fear for his life.

I don't think Jacob liked being sent away from his comfortable situation at home. Perhaps he, too, vowed that when he had a family, he would do things differently. And even though his family life began differently from his father's and his grandfather's, it ended up being the same. One of the differences was that he married two wives, Leah and Rachel. He didn't intend it that way—Laban set him up. And Jacob chose to favor one wife and reject the other. Over the years the wife he rejected, Leah, bore him one son after another—a sure way in that culture to gain your husband's favor. But it didn't affect Jacob's feelings—Rachel was his favorite, even though she was barren. When she finally had a son of her own, both she and Jacob favored Joseph and continued to reject the others.

As a result of his parents' favoritism, Joseph became a spoiled brat. He was arrogant, grandiose, and so naive he didn't even know that his brothers hated him. Finally, the resentment of Joseph's brothers grew until, one day in the fields, they threw him into a pit with the intent to murder him. His life was preserved only when God sent the slave traders along and his brothers chose to sell him instead of kill him. This was the third generation of Abraham's family. The pattern of chronic rejection and favoritism had intensified so that, once again, one son was sent away, and this time he barely escaped being murdered by his brothers.

Three generations in this godly family, where one child was favored and others were rejected. Each generation experienced the same results—one son was sent away. Patterns of rejection and favoritism require a price from both the rejected and the favored. Unless someone outside the family steps in to balance out the dysfunction, distortions in our belief systems and Self-Talk become ingrained and will set us up to act in ways that only seem to guarantee the repetition of destructive patterns. Vowing to do it differently seems impotent to change the past. Something more is obviously required.

A Major Traumatic Experience

Not all of us may identify with the issue of boundary violations or of chronic rejection during our growing up years. But many of us can remember a traumatic event when we feared for ourselves or for someone we loved. We may have developed fear-based ways of thinking and behaving that arose out of one or more traumatic events in our lives.

Gary's mother was sick for several years during his adolescence. She seemed to endlessly hover on the edge of death. During this time of great anxiety, Gary developed a pattern of compulsively needing to touch a light switch whenever he passed one as he walked through the house. "I felt that if I failed to touch even one light switch," Gary said, "that failure would cause my mother to die." Gary had found a way to relieve his anxieties through his compulsiveness, but over time and even after his mother had recovered, his anxieties became focused on his compulsive behaviors. He spent more and more time needing to touch the light switch as he walked by and would often have to retrace his steps to make certain he did it right. His mother was no longer the issue, but the obsessive-compulsive patterns that were used to alleviate his anxiety regarding his mother's possible death had now taken on a life of their own. Each day, much of his thinking and behaving was centered around these patterns.

Sometimes we can be deeply affected by something that occurs within the larger context of our extended family or even within our neighborhood, especially if we didn't feel that our parents were really able to protect us in the situation. For example, we may have lost a sibling while we were young, and our parents were so grieved that they had little left to give us or to help us deal with our own grief. Or a friend may have been confronted by an exhibitionist, and our parents, reacting with extreme fear, severely restricted our own activities out of concern that the same thing could happen to us.

In both these examples, the parents were so overwhelmed by their own pain or fears that they were unable to provide a sense of safety for us. This left us feeling vulnerable and anxious, and it increased the impact of these traumatic events in shaping our thoughts and beliefs about ourselves and our safety in the world.

Distorted Beliefs of Parents

Sometimes our growing up years are uneventful, but the distortions, or limitations, of our parents and our family in their own conversations may have shaped our own belief systems and Self-Talk. One of our parents may have, almost obsessively, focused only on certain topics while at the same time completely ignoring more important issues, such as drug abuse by a family member or conflict within the marriage.

Charlie's parents did this. He remembers that when his older brother started abusing drugs and dropped out of school, nothing was ever discussed in the family. Dinner conversations focused on the problems at the church with the pastor and how he should resign before the church died. For several years, both his parents seemed obsessed about the pastor problems at the church while at the same time ignoring the problems with his brother. Charlie's attempts to compensate for his parental distortions created an opposite distortion for him with his children—problems at the church were never to be discussed, especially at the dinner table. Parental distortions will often create either the same distortions within our thought patterns or reactive distortions within us as we go to the opposite extreme, as Charlie did.

We are also taught other things by example, such as the belief that talking about certain things within our family is forbidden. For many of us, anger was forbidden in children but permitted in adults. If we got angry as a child, we were punished and sent to our room until we could "act normal." But our parents could be angry all the time. What we saw in the behavior of our parents in particular was completely at odds with what they said to us.

Our purpose in looking at the experiences we had within our family of origin is to show that patterns of behavior and thought deeply influence the development of the basic beliefs we have about ourselves, about others, about the world, about God, and about the nature of relationships. We become stuck in self-defeating patterns of thinking and talking because of the distortions we hold onto. We do it through our inner dialogue with ourselves—our Self-Talk. And we are usually drawn toward other people who will not challenge our thought distortions, which serves only to reinforce them and make them more difficult to challenge and change.

What Shaped *My* Self-Talk?

Over the years I've talked with some people who have worked hard on their Self-Talk and become very frustrated in their attempts to break destructive patterns in their thoughts and words. In each case when I've had an opportunity to talk with them, I've found that there were one or more of the dysfunctional patterns we've just described in their childhood. Breaking free from their distorted Self-Talk required them to better understand their family of origin and its influence in their lives.

The words of Isaiah quoted at the beginning of this chapter tell us where we go when we want to experience change in our lives. He invites each of us "who hope for deliverance, who seek the Lord" to look at our roots, to look to our ancestors. To us he says, "Consider the quarry from which you were mined, the rock from which you were cut!" I remember a number of times while growing up when my father's friends would look at me and say, "Well, he's a chip off the old block!" If I'm going to understand me, I need to understand the "block" from which I was chipped. We all need to understand our roots.

To help you "consider the quarry from which you were mined, the rock from which you were cut," here is a list of questions for you to think through and answer.

Beliefs about Myself

How would you have described yourself as a child? As a teenager?

What did you like about yourself? What didn't you like?

How did you think others your age perceived you as a child? As a teenager? How did you think adults perceived you?

What were you good at? Not so good at?

What were some things about you or your circumstances that you wished you could have changed when you were a child? A teenager?

What are some of the things you say or think about yourself that you've "always" said about yourself?

What are some of the things you remember being told about your intellect? About your appearance? About your friends?

About your abilities? (Think of both positives and negatives, if possible.)

How do you handle compliments today?

Who do you trust today? Why?

Beliefs about Others

Write down three adjectives that describe your mother; three that describe your father; three that describe each of your siblings.

As a child, what do you remember thinking about adults? About your teachers? About other kids? About parents in general?

What were some of your parents' beliefs about other people that you remember hearing them say while you were growing up?

Who were your favorite adults? Why?

Finish this statement: I still feel intimidated when I am in the presence of . . .

Beliefs about the World

When you think about the future, what do you see?

When you think about the past, what do you try to avoid remembering?

What do you like best/least about the world we live in today? While growing up?

What do you think needs to be remedied in our world?

What current political issues do you support? Which ones do you not support? Why? Are you repeating a pattern from your family, or are you reacting against a pattern from your family?

Beliefs about God

What is the hardest thing for you to *experience* in your relationship with God today?

How is that struggle similar to feelings you had about your parents while you were growing up?

Finish this sentence: I wish God were more . . .

Other Beliefs

How did your family handle conflicts?

What do you wish had been different in the way your family members related to each other?

What was discussed often within your family? What is it that was never talked about?

When you were upset as a child or teenager, what did you usually do in order to feel better?

If something in your family upset you, what did you usually do?

Who talked in your family? Who didn't talk?

If your family had an "attitude," how would you have described it? Or you might think of it as a "family motto" that was often repeated, whether true or not. What could have been your family motto when you were growing up?

As you think through these questions, the purpose is to be able to better identify some of the deep belief systems you picked up while growing up and which are the foundation of your Self-Talk today.

Distortions in your current perception of yourself are based on experiences accumulated over your lifetime in relationships with people you considered important or powerful. If you received rejection messages from your parents while growing up, you have developed over the years a whole strategy of thought patterns that help you carefully scan your environment for any sign of rejection. You are probably more than willing to blame yourself or to absorb blame messages from others in order to avoid outright rejection. Your concerns about your inadequacies and shortcomings may lead you to overeat as a way to compensate for all these negative messages about yourself, which in turn only reinforces the negative feelings you have about yourself.

Adults who had their personal boundaries violated as a child through sexual molestation will develop thought patterns in which they blame themselves for what happened. One young woman was convinced that the reason her brother molested her when she was five and six years old was because at five she "danced provocatively" in front of him. For years she berated herself in her Self-Talk for causing this horrible thing to happen to her. When I asked her how a five-year-old decides to be provocative sexually, she said, "Now that you ask me, I know it's not true, but I've always had those thoughts."

In addition, when we have distorted messages about ourselves we will often sift through all the statements being made to us to find only those that support our distortions. In this young woman, years of sexual fidelity as an adult were minimized and a brief encounter with a young man as a teenager, in which nothing happened except the desire for something to happen, was blown out of proportion. She greatly exaggerated her lustful desire to "prove" that she was responsible for her molestation.

Not all distortions are stated in the negative. Sometimes we distort our self-perceptions by accentuating a positive that isn't really a positive. For example, we may think and say about ourselves that "I don't get upset by things that happen to me like others do." Or, "I'm pretty easygoing." Or, "I'm not worried about how the boss sees me. I'm too valuable to the company for them to do anything." In each of these statements there is an element of denial that makes it a distortion. Even though it is in a so-called positive direction, it is nonetheless dangerous because we are excusing something in ourselves that needs to be looked at more carefully. The fact that I am easygoing can be good at times, but there are other times when I may simply use that description of myself to dismiss some conflict with another person. In reality, I end up acting irresponsibly. The man who feels he is so valuable to the company that he doesn't need to worry about how his boss perceives him will probably lose not only that job but will also have a string of jobs he has lost because of his attitude.

Quite often these distortions we have of ourselves that appear to be positive are the things our parents said about us as they excused our irresponsibility. Every thought that goes through our mind needs to be examined—nothing is exempt, even when the thought seems so positive.

Importance of Knowing

The purpose of this chapter is really twofold. First, it is important that we become aware of the roots of our Self-Talk. Enhanced awareness is always the first and most essential ingredient for any meaningful change in life. Jeremiah says that "you can't heal a wound by saying it's not there!" (Jer. 6:14 TLB). In the case of our Self-Talk, increased awareness of our belief systems' roots will begin to shake the foundation of faulty beliefs and create room for more accurate, biblically based beliefs.

Second, this chapter is especially important for those who will try some of the exercises in the following chapters and who will find themselves increasingly frustrated by their failure to break their patterns of destructive Self-Talk. If, as you work through the following chapters, you find yourself increasingly frustrated over time because it seems like no matter how hard you work at it, nothing is changing, go back over this chapter and look carefully at how your family of origin has affected your life. The key to change is found in understanding our past.

Sometimes we resist looking at our past because we are afraid that in some way we will be dishonoring our parents. The search for the truth, as long as it is our search together with God, never requires that we dishonor those who raised us. In fact, distorting our memory of those early years through either denial or idealizing is what really dishonors the past, because it makes the past unreal. We must become fearless in our search for the truth, knowing that the truth does indeed set us free. But the search for the truth is never an excuse to blame or to confront—it's *our* search, and its purpose lies within us.

Questions for Personal Growth and Discussion

1. When you looked at the various distorted thoughts you learned growing up, which was distorted more in your family background: distortions about yourself, about others, about the world, about God? In what ways?

2. What words or thought patterns have you caught yourself saying or thinking that are "just like Mom or Dad"?

3. What was the major family pattern that shaped your Self-Talk?

FIVE

Self-Talk and Anger

Do you do well to be angry?

Jonah 4:4

Anger can be witty or just plain catty; it can take the form of a clever remark or a verbal sock in the stomach. But the most commonly identified form of anger is the exploding temper. We struggle with that form of anger because it seems so childish. Adults, after all, are to be more subtle and clever in expressing anger.

Perhaps that's why we have so much trouble with anger. Many of us are very angry but almost totally unaware of it. Others are angry and know it but feel trapped because they don't know how to get rid of those feelings. They try to pretend they have no anger, but there is chaos within. A major internal riot threatens to erupt at the slightest provocation.

A lot of us are confused about anger because somewhere along the way we were taught that anger should not exist in our lives. We need to be reassured that anger is a perfectly valid and natural human emotion. There are times when we have every reason to feel angry. People let us down; someone tries to hurt us or our family; we hear on the news about a child beaten to death by one of his parents; or we see a picture of children dying of starvation. We need to feel that anger. Accept it, for it is part of our emotional makeup put there by God.

"But," some of you protest, "I don't ever get angry!" If you feel that way, be assured that my intention is not to turn you into an angry person. However, if anger is a valid human emotion, and you say you don't ever get angry, then you are missing part of life. Our religious training has prompted many of us to deny the existence of anger. "Righteous indignation" was acceptable for Jesus—and perhaps for us in extreme situations—but not anger! So to help you understand this chapter and perhaps understand your emotions better, you could simply change the word *anger* to *annoyance, frustration,* or *irritation.*

Be Angry but Sin Not

I think the one person who struggled with anger even more than we do was the apostle Paul. I see Paul really wrestling with anger, because he was basically an angry man.

When we first meet Paul as Saul, we meet a man who is enraged at the Christian church. It could be called righteous indignation by a fellow Jew; but in reality Paul is extremely angry.

As Saul becomes Paul through the new birth, he is faced with the destructiveness of his anger. He has vivid memories of how he could lose control of his anger. So as he writes to the young churches, he consistently warns them of the dangers associated with anger. He tells the Colossians to "put them all away: anger, wrath, malice, slander, and foul talk from your mouth" (Col. 3:8).

Perhaps the best insight into how Paul felt about anger is seen in his letter to the Galatians. Notice where he lists anger: "Now the works of the flesh are plain: immorality, impurity, licentiousness, idolatry, sorcery, enmity, strife, jealousy, anger, selfishness, dissension, party spirit, envy, drunkenness, carousing, and the like" (see Gal. 5:19–21). We are, according to Paul, to get rid of anger! Everything else on the list is behavior or an attitude; anger is the only emotion listed. And we're not to allow anything on the list to be a part of our life.

Paul is deeply concerned with this emotion. Part of his struggle is due to the fact that he is a devout Jew, a Pharisee. As such, he knows the Old Testament well. I don't know if he ever counted the number of times the word *anger* is used in the Old Testament, but someone he knew probably had and told him. There are over 450 places in the Old Testament where the word *anger* is used. Over 75 percent of these references relate to God's anger. The other references often involve the anger of the great men of faith in the Old Testament.

To complicate Paul's struggle is the reality of Jesus's anger. Jesus showed anger a number of times. For example, in Mark 3 his anger is very clear:

> Again he entered the synagogue, and a man was there who had a withered hand. And they watched him, to see whether he would heal him on the sabbath, so that they might accuse him. And he said to the man who had the withered hand, "Come here." And he said to them, "Is it lawful on the sabbath to do good or to do harm, to save life or to kill?" But they were silent. *And he looked around at them with anger,* grieved at their hardness of heart, and said to the man, "Stretch out your hand." He stretched it out, and his hand was restored.
>
> Mark 3:1–5, italics added

Now how does Paul reconcile his ideas about anger and these examples? He says that anger is the work of the flesh—sin. But God's anger punctuates the Old Testament, and Jesus was obviously angry at times. Paul must have struggled with how anger could be so evil in light of these facts.

Use your imagination to picture how Paul must have stewed over that dilemma. He is in prison and is busily writing a letter to the Ephesian Christians. Perhaps something happens during the day that makes Paul very angry. All of the struggles with his anger come to the surface of his mind, and as he attempts to sleep, he tosses and turns fitfully. Suddenly, he sits up, wide awake.

"Aha!" he shouts, "I've got it!" as he wakes everyone up, including his scribe, Tychicus. Paul is excited. He asks Tychicus to write something down. "I've got another thought I want in that letter we were writing." And he tells Tychicus to write, "Be angry but do not sin!" Sometimes I imagine that Paul quickly falls back to sleep, while his scribe is awake the rest of the night trying to figure out what Paul meant.

One almost wants to join Tychicus and wake Paul up demanding, "What do you mean by that?" The first time I read that verse I thought to myself, "That feels so good! Now I can get angry." But then I wondered how I could get angry and not sin. Of course, when I became angry at first, I didn't worry about the not sinning part. All I knew was that it felt good to be angry, at least at the time.

It's only afterward that we begin to feel bad about what we said or did in our anger. That's why we get stuck in the same struggle as Paul. Anger feels good, for it is a genuine human emotion. But the results of our being angry often throw us into the same confusion we experienced earlier when we thought that all anger was wrong.

Paul appears to be one who would fall into the area of over-controlling his anger. If we take the grid we made in the first chapter, we can put Paul in the lower right-hand section of the grid. He was certainly aware of his feelings of anger, but based on his previous experiences, Paul tried to deny the existence of anger in his life.

When we get caught in that overcontrolling reaction to anger, we find ourselves in the same place as Paul—aware of the feeling of anger but working hard at denying it. This is shown on the grid below. When we find ourselves in this spot, we force a smile on our face, grit our teeth, and say something like, "Who's angry? Not me!" while inside our emotions are tearing us apart.

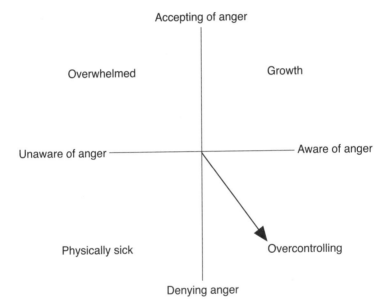

On the other hand, we can see that if we accept our anger but are unaware of its existence until too late, we can easily become caught in a pattern of being overwhelmed by our anger. This is shown in the grid on the next page.

When we are caught in this spot, we will lose our temper, scream at the kids, or slam doors. This venting of anger may prevent us from getting ulcers, but it probably transfers that possibility to those on the receiving end of our anger.

When we can accept our anger and be aware of its source as it develops within us, we are able to deal effectively with both our anger and its cause. Then we are in the quadrant of growth.

Picture where you are on the grid. Do you have problems accepting the emotion of anger? Do you have difficulty identifying your anger before it's too late? If you struggle with both accepting and being aware of your anger, you are setting up a pattern that can create all kinds of physical problems. Anger is the killer emotion. To deny or be unaware of anger not only wears us out emotionally, it wears us down physically, leaving us vulnerable to all kinds of diseases.

What does happen when we get angry? What goes on inside our bodies? A look at *Webster's New World Dictionary* gives us a starting point and provides some interesting insight. The word

anger is derived from the base *angh-*, which means "constricted, narrow, tightness, and distress." A few entries further down on the same page, the word *angina* is defined as any localized spasm of pain. It is derived from the base *angh-*, just as in anger, which links anger and angina. Even in ancient times, when language was still being developed, people saw a connection between what they were experiencing physically and the emotion of anger.

The early research on anger focused primarily on this physical side. One of the first studies showed a wide variety of physical symptoms. People said that they felt either hot or cold, clenched their fists, and experienced sweating, choking, numbness, or twitching. Some people said they felt flush, while others said they felt pale. Some reported that their anger made them feel more alive and alert, while others said it made them feel afraid and even gave them headaches or nosebleeds.

Another early study observed the physical reactions in animals when they became afraid or angry. Both emotions caused physical changes. Digestion, assimilation, and elimination halted as the blood vessels to the stomach and intestines constricted, cutting off blood flow to these areas. Blood flow increased in the areas important in carrying out any decisions made as a result of anger: the brain, heart, lungs, and larger muscles in the arms and legs.

Researchers today have more sophisticated equipment available to help them in their study. Blood pressure, blood counts, brain waves, skin temperature, and heart rate are recorded in order to see what happens in the body when a person becomes angry. Some of these findings are summarized in an article in the June 1979 issue of *Changing Times:*

> Consider the caveman. The sight of an enemy or dangerous animal
> sets off a series of hormonal and physical reactions. Adrenaline

pours into his blood, speeding up his heartbeat and raising his blood pressure. Available fuel entering the blood as sugar increases, the red cells flood his bloodstream to transport more oxygen to the muscles and brain. Breathing accelerates to supply additional oxygen and to eliminate carbon dioxide created by sudden activity. Blood ordinarily required for digestion is shunted to the brain and muscles. Digestion slows. Pupils dilate, improving vision. Blood clotting ability accelerates, preparing for the possibility of a wound. All this gears the caveman for action to protect himself. In this aroused state he can stay and fight if the odds look good or flee if they don't.

Our bodies react the same way, though the danger is more likely to be a letter from the IRS than a saber-toothed tiger. And the threat doesn't have to be immediate to cause arousal. Merely anticipate anything unpleasant, perplexing or uncertain, and you can feel the stress reaction go off inside.[1]

The article could have added that all or part of the physical reactions described for short-term emergencies can become an ongoing response to life as a result of repressed anger. Eventually, if we continue to bury our anger, the physical responses of long-term anger can create a breakdown within our bodies. Depending on our physical makeup, we may find ourselves suffering from any number of illnesses, ranging from mild elimination problems to hypertension or even cancer. It is only recently that we are finding out that anger can trigger other physical illnesses besides the occasional headache or an ulcer.

Both anger and fear are healthy emotions. They serve as warning systems that protect us from impending danger. But these two emotions, when left unresolved, can create physical damage to our bodies in the form of illness. When we look again at our love-anger-fear cycle, we see that two of the three are factors in the development of disease.

Building on the research of Dr. Meyer Friedman, which identified Type A behavior as a cause of heart disease, and the work of Dr. Carl Simonton in his research on cancer, doctors have come to realize that unresolved anger and fear play a role in both of these major killers. In fact, researchers are finding that, except in the case of a trauma such as a car accident or some other accidental injury, anger and fear play a role in almost all the physical damage done to our bodies. A specialist in psychosomatic illnesses, Harvard psychiatrist Dr. Silverman insists that a person cannot get sick without a stress factor being involved. He identifies the buried emotions of anger and fear as the most important stress factors in physical illness.

What role do germs play in physical illnesses then? Are they not the real cause of disease? What about the effects of air pollution and the carcinogenic particles that are supposed to cause cancer—where do they fit in? And what effect does diet have—isn't it an important factor? All of these are still important factors in illness, but they are not the critical factors. In studies done with identical twins who have the same genetic tendency toward an illness, or with people who breathe the same air or take into their bodies the same carcinogenic particles or eat the same diet—one might get sick while the other will not. The one who gets sick is generally the one exposed to an emotionally stressful situation in which overwhelming feelings of anger or fear are ignored.

Because of the personal emotional investment we make in marriage, unresolved feelings of anger and fear in that relationship can make it one of the most stressful situations we can experience. Unless we find some way to effectively resolve these feelings, they can build to such an intensity that they can cause Type A behavior in any one of us. With Type A behavior, coronary heart disease can easily erupt in one's thirties or forties. Some people call Type A behavior the "hurry sickness" and feel that in order to avoid dealing with our feelings of anger or fear, we jump onto the treadmill of life. If we can go faster, we won't have to deal with anything. Because of this drive to get things done, or the continual time pressures we create, we simply add more things to be angry about—the cycle is complete. The faster we go, the more things we have to ignore. The more things we ignore, the more we experience anger or fear, and the faster we have to go in order to avoid these emotions. Medical researchers now identify this cycle as part of Type A behavior and see that any treatment plan must include the treatment of anger and fear if the healing process is to be complete.

What Dr. Friedman discovered about Type A behavior and heart disease, Dr. Carl Simonton has found to be equally true with cancer patients. The first trait that he and his team of researchers found to be at the root of cancer is a great tendency to hold in resentment and anger. In treating cancer patients, Dr. Simonton combines conventional medical treatment with psychotherapy. He and his associates insist on the psychotherapy in order to deal with buried anger. Often they see amazing remission of the disease as the person begins to deal effectively with that anger.

Another researcher, Dr. Robert Good, has shown that cancer cells develop within each of us on a daily basis. But we do not develop the disease of cancer because the body's white cells stay busy as they continually attack and destroy these cancer cells before they can fully mature and take hold. The reason some people do develop cancer, according to Good, is the presence of emotional stressors, particularly unresolved anger. The hormones that the body releases under prolonged stress, including the hormone adrenaline, inhibit the body's normal ability to fight and destroy the cancer cells.

Simonton goes even further when he asserts that all illness, ranging from cancer to the common cold or a stomachache, is a result of the interaction of our bodies, our minds, and our emotions. According to him, the path to health and wellness begins when we take responsibility for our sickness. In order to do this, we must begin to work through the buried emotions of fear and anger. That's not a comfortable concept. We may be able to help others work through their anger in order to prevent illness, but working through our own anger is another matter. That's probably why it stays hidden so long.

So it is clear that repressing anger—keeping it buried in the dark corners of our memory—is not a healthy way to handle that emotion. Yet we continue to avoid our anger, even though we can clearly see that that behavior is uproductive. But what is our alternative? Does expressing our anger, or letting it all hang out, provide better results? If burying anger doesn't work, then let's lay it out on the table and see how that works.

The Myths of Anger

Freud encouraged us in this direction. He said that we walk around with our conscious mind knowing less than half of what we are doing or why we are doing it. Our unconscious mind is really in control, and that deep, dark part of us is a churning cauldron of destructive impulses battling anything good within us. Those destructive impulses feed on our repressed emotions.

Freud saw aggression as a central part of our nature. At every stage of human development, we are supposed to be *enraged* at someone. Although he seldom said anything about anger directly, his ideas have filtered into our minds so that we link anger with aggression. His followers have come along and portrayed anger as the driving force behind most forms of aggression. They point out that anger is the emotion we feel when we have those aggressive impulses. These theorists imply that if people do not become aggressive when angry, it is only because they are too inhibited to act out their aggressiveness.

Freud believed that when the emotion of anger comes to the surface of the unconscious and we become aware of it, we still do our best to push it back down. We do not want to face our repressed emotions. Some feel that perhaps we do this because we have been taught by example to avoid our anger, or we have learned through painful and embarrassing experiences how dangerous our anger can become. Keeping anger in the unconscious may work for a short period of time, but eventually anger seems to fester and explode when we least expect it. This has led theorists to encourage us to become aware of our anger and get it out on the table before it can explode.

Although Freud was speaking about aggression metaphorically, many of his ideas have been taken literally. One of the most familiar concepts is the "hydraulic" theory of anger. This theory assumes that stored emotions become like a hydraulic system, something like the brakes on a car. When you push on one area, something has to give in another. Stored-up anger will come bursting out in some unpredictable manner when someone pushes us the wrong way.

Closely related to the hydraulic theory is the "reservoir" theory. This approach maintains that when we repress an emotion like anger, it is stored up in some huge reservoir. Unless we find some way to let out our anger, it will grow to enormous proportions, seeping or bursting out of the reservoir of the unconscious at the most inappropriate time, ruining some important relationship.

Although these ideas sound logical, and may even feel right, they have never been supported by the results of research. In spite of this, many counselors ignore this lack of empirical support and tell their clients that it is dangerous to dam up any feelings because this may cause them to spill over, either in the form of neurotic or other inappropriate behavior.

Some of the leaders in popular psychology have taken these ideas a step further and have encouraged us to "ventilate" our emotions, particularly the emotion of anger. The hydraulic theory and the reservoir theory are rather passive ways of handling our emotions—the feelings just overflow all by themselves. But ventilating our emotions is a more active method, which advises, "Don't just let it seep out, actively do something to release the tension!" Expressions like "let it all hang out" are an encouragement to let the anger out. If we could only actively ventilate our anger in some way, we might be able to get rid of that anger; we might experience catharsis. It seems like a reasonable set of ideas: if damming up our anger causes it to fester and grow, then actively ventilating our anger should cause it to diminish.

A whole range of behaviors has been identified as being cathartic: vigorous physical activity, such as running, exercise, or sports; throwing dishes; beating pillows; fantasizing revenge; or even kicking a stone. It is believed that if you can experience the release of physical energy through these behaviors, you can also experience release from pent-up anger. Even the National Association for Mental Health advocates this type of behavior. One of their suggestions for resolving stressful emotions is, "Work off your anger. Cool it for a day or two while expending physical energy in a do-it-yourself project around the house, playing tennis, or taking long walks." Unfortunately, when we try to let go of anger through physical release, we usually end up still angry.

Some of the advocates of ventilating anger add another dimension in their approach. They have changed the cry of "Express yourself" to "Look out for number one!" If you are looking out for yourself, ventilating anger can feel pretty good. "I feel so much better" is the testimony of those who have just expressed their anger. But check back later and you will find the anger still hanging around. Of course, some people are not too concerned with several days from now or that the problem still remains—all that matters is that they feel better.

The idea of expressing anger, or ventilating it, is not new in this generation. Its roots go way back in time. Aristotle tried to help orators control angry audiences when they shouted back at a speaker they disagreed with. William Blake, the eighteenth-century English poet and artist, wrote a poem, "The Poison Tree," that expressed some of the ideas of the ventilationists. He wrote:

> I was angry with my friend;
> I told my wrath, my wrath did end.
> I was angry with my foe;
> I told it not, my wrath did grow.

Blake was a good poet and even a good philosopher for the ventilationist school of thinking, but he overlooked some of the same things the advocates of ventilating anger also overlook. Sometimes there are situations in which we want to hide our wrath from a friend because the value of that friendship far outweighs the importance of what made us angry. Does that mean our wrath will not end? Or what about the situation where in our rage we express our wrath to a foe, who also happens to outweigh us by a hundred pounds? Expressing anger in that situation just might increase the other person's anger to the point of endangering our physical well-being. The poem, along with the advice of the ventilationists, doesn't always fit with our experiences.

In spite of these inconsistencies, the ventilationists would lead us to believe that not only do we clear our arteries when we express our anger, we help to improve the quality of our relationships as well. Marriage counselors are quick to jump on the bandwagon and tell couples that it is healthy for them to express their anger to each other. But in marriage after marriage, the outcome is the same—the angry outburst is followed by louder and louder accusations, then crying or screaming, until one or both people give up through sheer exhaustion. Then one may offer a reluctant apology, or both may just settle into a moody silence that is a welcomed relief from the shouting. But the silence is only a quiet recess, for the next day, or several days or weeks later, the scene is repeated. Nothing is changed. Nobody really feels any better, and neither the problem nor the anger has gone away.

Most of the advocates of the ventilation theory would never advocate screaming matches. That is what is called "dirty fighting." Instead, they seek to control the expression of anger, seeing it as a helpful form of communication. Expressing our anger means we say to our spouse something like, "Get out of my way—I'm looking for a fight." Whether this is stated verbally or is expressed through nonverbal behavior, it hardly sounds like a constructive form of communication.

The point overlooked by the ventilationists is that merely expressing anger does nothing to effectively resolve it. Study after study shows that only when the expression of anger leads directly to a resolution of the root problem does this type of behavior lead to a reduction of anger.

Some of the "milder" advocates among the ventilationists attempt to pull us closer to what they see as the center of the spectrum. They say the solution is to "talk over your anger." That sounds like a reasonable form of expressing anger. Talking things over with a sympathetic listener, such as a good friend, should make one feel better. But once again, these theorists end up in another blind alley, for they overlook the fact that efforts to talk through anger are really efforts to justify our point of view. That's why talking out anger with a friend, or even with a therapist, seldom reduces anger. Instead, it causes us to rehearse in our mind the situation that originally triggered the anger. This in turn can give us a clearer picture of why we feel justified in our anger. And we end up just as angry, or perhaps even more so than before, because we have received support for our cause.

The next time you try to talk out your anger with a friend, notice what you are feeling as you talk with your sympathetic listener. Notice what happens each time she agrees with you. As you talk through your anger, you will probably become aware of more of the nuances surrounding the anger-triggering event. Your sympathetic listener nods her head in agreement, not only with what you are feeling but also with your right to feel that anger. Your anger becomes more defined, and in turn, you may even begin to feel angrier than you did when you started to talk through it.

The same thing can happen when you attempt to talk through your anger with your spouse. In this situation, instead of receiving sympathy from your listener, you will probably receive a defensive statement—one in which your partner defends his right to act the way he did, or say what he said. The more he defends his right to behave as he did, the more you have to defend your right to be angry. The result is more and more anger.

Whatever our style of dealing with anger, most of us find it easy to be angry and to sin. The reason is that we get caught in the same $A = C$ type of thinking. We say the reason for our anger is that something's happened to us to make us angry. This is even seen in the dictionary definition of *anger:* "a feeling of displeasure resulting from injury, mistreatment, opposition, etc., and usually showing itself in a desire to fight back at the supposed cause of this feeling." A clear example of that definition is when we say or think, "He makes me so angry!"

Of course, we demonstrated in chapter 2 that the activating events in our lives do not cause our emotional consequences. *A* does not cause *C*. Therefore *you* can't make me angry! Only our own thoughts—our Self-Talk—can create within us the emotion of anger. Since we make the choices about what we think, we are the ones who make the choice to be angry.

When you understand what happens in your Self-Talk that leads you to choose to be angry, you are on your way to finding out how you can be angry and not sin. The way you do that is to look at the *B*—your belief systems. What are you saying and believing about what is happening that causes you to be angry?

Whenever we become angry, we have initial feelings of hurt, frustration, or implied threat that we need to pay attention to. But when we get over those initial feelings and still feel angry, it is because we are making demands on another person or situation. For example, a wife spends all afternoon preparing a special dinner. She sets the table with the best dishes, picks up some flowers for the center of the table, and puts out the candlesticks. Husband comes home, and it's been one of those days. He grunts a greeting, grabs the paper, turns on the TV news, and hides in his lounger-chair. Well, in about five minutes or less, depending on how often this happens, they are going at each other full steam! The air is filled with anger! And after the dinner has burned, the candles have melted, and the wife wipes her eyes dry, it's probably not the best time to point out to her that it was her thoughts that made her angry! "But he . . ." kinds of statements could go on for hours. The fact remains the same, though—it is her thoughts that make her angry.

Imagine what she's thinking to herself, statements such as:

He does this every time I prepare a special dinner!

He should know how hard I worked this afternoon!

Why can't he at least talk to me and tell me he's tired?

What an awful way to treat me!

Husbands shouldn't be so insensitive.

Look at all the nice things I did for him! He should know how much I did without me telling him!

He better shape up or else!

There's an "obscene" word in some of those statements that ties in to the basic cause of anger. That word is *should*. Every time you feel frustration or hurt that leads to anger, you can connect your anger to the *shoulds* in your Self-Talk. The shoulds always reflect a *demand* that you are making on another person or on life and the world. Of course, these shoulds can be expressed in a negative way as *shouldn'ts*—with the same effect.

Other words are derivatives of the shoulds, words like *must, gotta, ought to,* and so forth. They all do the same thing—trigger anger. And they do this because we are making a demand on a situation or person, a demand that we cannot effectively guarantee will be met. And that's the source of our anger.

Sometimes the shoulds are implied by what is left unstated. The thoughts of the wife who prepared the special dinner say, "He does this every time I prepare a special dinner!" What she doesn't say, but which is certainly in her mind, is, "And he shouldn't do that!" Why is she making that demand? Why do we make those kinds of demands on other people and on life? We really have no way to make sure that they will ever stop doing that. So when we set up these demands within our Self-Talk, we create an emotional tension within that takes the form of anger.

Get Rid of the Demands

Do you feel angry? Look for the shoulds or shouldn'ts. The key to defusing your anger is to identify these demands and change them into wants and desires.

Let's look at that wife again. The same scene recurs some days later. Only this time the wife is aware of the effect of her shoulds. So instead of making those demands on her husband in her Self-Talk, she creates Self-Talk in the form of wants and desires. Now she says and thinks things like:

I wish he'd notice all the work I've done.

I don't like the way he acts when he comes home. Perhaps I can take the time to talk with him first.

If he doesn't notice, I'll survive. Wish he would.

Life would be more pleasant if he'd find another way to relax when he comes home.

You might read over this list and the other list of thoughts to see if they create a different type of feeling inside of you. The second list still does not guarantee that the wife will get what she wants. But it certainly reduces the tension level, and that frees some emotional energy to find creative ways to deal with the situation.

Moses is a good example of what we are talking about. In Exodus 32 he is on the mountain talking with God. God tells him he'd better get back to the camp, for the Israelites are making an idol. And God is angry. He tells Moses, "Let me alone, that my wrath may burn hot against them" (v. 10). But Moses pleads with God, and God turns away from his anger.

Then Moses goes down from the mountain, carrying the two tablets of stone on which were written the Ten Commandments. In verse 16 we read that "the tables were the work of God, and the writing was the writing of God."

As Moses nears the camp, he hears the people shouting. "And as soon as he came near the camp and saw the calf and the dancing, Moses' *anger burned hot,* and he threw the tables out of his hands and broke them at the foot of the mountain. And he took the calf which they had made, and burnt it with fire, and ground it to powder, and scattered it upon the water, and made the people of Israel drink it" (vv. 19–20, italics added). Here is a man overwhelmed with his emotions—his anger burned hot! That's real anger.

But look what he does. He breaks the tablets that were written by God. And then he not only destroys the golden calf, he makes the people drink the ashes of that idol. He is mad! Now that isn't really an appropriate response. Especially when he has to climb back up the mountain and get a new set of tablets. It must have felt good at the moment, but it doesn't do him any good because Moses isn't really dealing with the cause of his anger. He thinks he is angry because of the awful things the people were doing. But the people keep doing these things, and Moses keeps struggling with his overwhelming emotion of anger. In Numbers 20 he loses his cool again. The people are being nasty—that's clear. They gripe and complain to the point that Moses has to go and talk to the Lord again. They need water, so God tells Moses to go and *speak* to the rock, and it will bring forth water.

But Moses' anger is strong. He heard what God said, but he is angry. So he gathers the people and says, "Hear now, you rebels; shall we bring forth water for you out of this rock?" (Num. 20:10). And then he lifts his rod and *strikes* the rock twice! It must have felt good to ventilate all that anger. But in God's eyes Moses was acting in angry disobedience and pride. As a result, God does not allow Moses to enter the Promised Land. How tragic! He misses entering the Promised Land because he never learns how to resolve his anger.

Now Moses can look back at thirty-eight years of hassles by the people. All they did was complain, and Moses was the one they complained to. So he can easily say, "They make me *so* angry!" Moses doesn't get sick over his anger—he doesn't develop an ulcer or arthritis. But he still pays a terrible price for venting his anger.

What Moses doesn't understand, apparently, is that the cause of his anger is right there inside him in the form of his Self-Talk. Imagine what he might have thought:

> God, why must I put up with these miserable people!
>
> I shouldn't have to listen to this!
>
> They're God's problem; I shouldn't have to take care of this!
>
> They should know better than to build an idol!
>
> I shouldn't have to fetch them water!
>
> I'll show them!

And the list could go on. Moses is making demands on the people, on God, on the life he has to live, and on himself. And he is powerless to guarantee that any of his demands can be met. Moses can make all the demands he wants, but it won't alter reality in any way. The idol has been made, the party is in progress, and the damage is already done! The same is true regarding the water in Numbers 20. His complaints are futile. And as inconvenient as it is, his demands in his Self-Talk will do nothing to change reality except make him angry.

Instead, Moses might have said in his Self-Talk something like:

God, I need more patience.

I'm really disappointed in Aaron and the people. I wish I could understand what happened.

Lord, I don't like this job, but with your help, I can survive.

I wish I had the Lord's patience with this water problem.

I wonder what it will take for these people to learn that God will provide.

Moses might be frustrated. He might feel disappointed. But his anger will be effectively controlled, because in his Self-Talk, he removes the irrational demands he is making on God, the people, and himself.

Peter is another example. In Matthew 26 Peter affirms his faithfulness to Jesus, only to be told that before the cock would crow he would deny his Lord three times.

When Jesus is arrested and taken to the high priest, Peter somehow stays close and watches it all. As every minute passes, his anger grows hotter. In his Self-Talk Peter probably says things like this:

Why does Jesus just stand there!

Why doesn't he bring lightning from the sky and get away!

Why doesn't God do something! He shouldn't let people treat his Son this way!

It's all so unfair!

Why didn't I try harder to protect him!

Peter's thoughts contain so many demands that he gets more and more angry. Then when someone standing nearby accuses Peter of being with Jesus, Peter denies it. Again, someone points to Peter, accusing him of being a follower of Jesus, and again, Peter denies the charge. The third time someone accuses Peter of being one of Jesus's disciples, Peter invokes a curse on himself and swears, "I do not know the man" (Matt. 26:74). Then the cock crows and Peter goes out and weeps bitterly. How he hurts. Obviously, being overwhelmed by his anger does not help him any more than it helps us. That's not the way to resolve anger!

The only way to resolve anger is to argue against the demands and then to change those demands into wants and desires. Argue against the shoulds. Argue against any type of demand on others or on life itself!

Peter, if he had argued with his Self-Talk, might have said or thought statements like these:

> I wish I had been braver!
>
> My heart is breaking with sadness! I wish I understood what is happening!
>
> I wish Jesus would do something. I know he could if he wanted to.
>
> Even though I don't understand, I still choose to believe that Jesus is the Christ, the Son of the living God!

If he had affirmed his faith and confidence in Almighty God, Peter's anger at what was occurring would have been under control.

But, you might be saying, that's no way to live. There should be some shoulds! Not if you want to resolve your anger! Or you might say, "There must be some shoulds." Well, the absence of shoulds seems to fit very nicely into what Jesus says in Matthew 5:38–45:

> You have heard that it was said, "An eye for an eye and a tooth for a tooth." But I say to you, Do not resist one who is evil. But if any one strikes you on the right cheek, turn to him the other also; and if any one would sue you and take your coat, let him have your cloak

as well; and if any one forces you to go one mile, go with him two miles. Give to him who begs from you, and do not refuse him who would borrow from you.

You have heard that it was said, "You shall love your neighbor and hate your enemy." But I say to you, Love your enemies and pray for those who persecute you, so that you may be sons of your Father who is in heaven; for he makes his sun rise on the evil and on the good, and sends rain on the just and on the unjust.

Don't resist, he says. Don't sit there and grovel in your anger; get up and go beyond the law. Even love your enemy, for the only thing that matters is to be the children of your Father. Don't worry about what is fair in life; no one ever said life would be fair. If that's true, then why do we sit around and get angry at the unfairness and injustices of life? Our anger only serves to paralyze us into inactivity or overwhelm us into saying or doing something that leads to hurt.

If someone strikes you and you make a demand in your Self-Talk that he shouldn't do that, you'll get angry. Jesus says to let that person hit you again. I don't think he means we're to stand there and tempt the other person to hit us again. That's foolishness. But I believe he is talking about an attitude of compromise and empathy. It is an attitude that does away with the demands, allowing them to exist only in the form of wants and desires. So instead of standing there saying:

You'd better not do that again.

You shouldn't have hit me.

I guess I must stand here and let him hit the other cheek as well.

what we are called to do is say in our Self-Talk things like:

I really wish he hadn't hit me.

That hurt. I'm getting out of here for now.

I wish I knew why he did that. He must be having some pain inside to do that to me.

Even though that kind of Self-Talk doesn't sound natural, that is what Jesus is saying here; and that type of Self-Talk will dissolve anger.

But shouldn't the other person stop hitting you? Of course. But placing demands on that person in your thoughts or even overtly in your speech is an irrational process. Why? For at least three reasons.

First, whenever we are angry about something with anyone, our shoulds are usually directed to the past. Notice what you said to yourself when you were using the word s*hould:* "You shouldn't have hit me." Can your demands on that person change the fact that he has already acted that way? Of course not. What is past is past. It can't be changed. But we can examine our Self-Talk and identify our shoulds and musts—the demands we are making related to the past. It is irrational to make demands on the past, because it cannot be changed. Our only choice, then, is to eliminate the demands.

But what about the future? He shouldn't act that way in the future! But notice what happens when you make that demand verbally on the other person. He'll probably say something like this:

Are you going to stop me?

Try and stop me.

Why shouldn't I?

And what are you going to do when that person responds like that? Get angry! Why? Because the second reason the demands are irrational is that you cannot enforce the demands you are making on another person about his future behavior. The result is that you are confronted with your own helplessness.

But what if the other person is really angry and makes some additional threats? Then you will probably experience the third reason why the demands are irrational: If you try to enforce your demands on the other person, you will encounter resistance. It seems to be human nature to resist the shoulds in life. We not only resist the ones placed on us by other people, we even resist the shoulds we place on ourselves. All shoulds are irrational! Only God can place a demand on us, for he's the only one who has the power to enforce the demand. People just don't have that kind of power.

You may still have some feelings of frustration, sadness, or even hurt. But those feelings do not paralyze you the way anger can if you don't resolve it. When you feel frustrated, sad, or hurt, you are still able to temper those feelings with compassion. And you are still able to act responsibly in the situation and even turn it into something constructive.

Here's a helpful way to organize your Self-Talk, to analyze your shoulds, and then to change your Self-Talk into wants and desires. On a big sheet of paper, make three columns. In the first column, make a list of some of the people and situations that trigger feelings of anger within you. In the second column, make a list of some of the shoulds or musts (the demands) you have attached to those persons or situations. Then, in the third column, rewrite those statements in the form of wants, wishes, or desires. For example:

Anger Triggers	Shoulds/Musts or Demands	Restated as Wants
My son loses his textbook.	He should know better. He should have taken care of it sooner. He should be more responsible. I shouldn't have to tell him.	I wish he'd act responsible. One of these days he will understand that he only hurts himself. I sure will be glad when he takes care of these things without my help.

Make the list as long as you can. Then every time you begin to feel angry about a particular situation, get the sheet out and read over the third column several times. After some practice, you will be able to do the same process within your mind, capturing every thought and bringing it into obedience. Look for the demands.

Remember, anger is part of being human. It is a basic and necessary emotion. Anger is like one of the warning lights on the dashboard of your car that says something isn't right. It demands your attention. If you ignore it, you're asking for all kinds of trouble. If you panic and are overwhelmed by that light, you can often complicate the problem. Instead, you can pay attention to the light and fix what is causing the light to go on. You "fix" anger by looking for the shoulds, arguing against those shoulds and demands, and changing them into wants and desires. Then you are able to be angry and not sin.

Questions for Personal Growth and Discussion

1. What were some of the attitudes you encountered about anger as you were growing up? How did they shape the way you deal with anger today?

2. What are some areas of anger in which you are having difficulty identifying the shoulds or the demands you are making on someone or on life?

3. Think of a relationship with someone you can change this week by changing your demands into wishes, wants, and desires. What is the first step you need to take?

SIX

Self-Talk and Depression

> But what am I?
> An infant crying in the night:
> An infant crying for the light:
> And with no language but a cry.
>
> Alfred, Lord Tennyson
> "In Memoriam"

For many of us, the problems we experience with anger and the corresponding irrational demands we make in our Self-Talk will eventually lead us directly into struggles with depression. One study suggested that during any given year, at least 15 percent of the adult population will suffer enough significant depressive symptoms that they should seek treatment.

Depression is big business, both in terms of psychiatric hospitalization (depression accounts for over three-fourths of all psychiatric hospitalizations) as well as in pharmacological sales and research. Drugs like Prozac, Paxill, Zoloft, and other designer antidepressants being developed represent billions of investment dollars that are aimed specifically at the treatment of depression. The costs of depression are compounded when we factor in the desperate price of suicides, most of which are caused by depression. It is the most unpleasant emotional experience people can have.

Depression is also a universal experience. Studies done in different countries around the world find that people in every culture experience depression. These studies have noted some contrasts in the way different peoples experience depression. For example, in the more primitive cultures studied, the emotional experience of depression is similar to ours, but the struggle with guilt is absent. Unlike what we experience in our Western culture, where our guilt causes us to blame ourselves, in these primitive cultures all blame is placed outside oneself. The forces of evil are the cause of one's problems. Since there is no self-blame, there is also no guilt. But the end result is the same—whether bad things happen to me because of some outside dark, evil force or because of my own foolishness, either way I am faced with my own helplessness and the despairing feelings of hopelessness.

Who, Me? Depressed?

Do people always know when they are depressed? Not always. We have a number of ways to avoid the reality of our own depression. Some people hide from it through constant busyness. They are on the go from the time they get up until the moment they drop exhausted into bed. Only when some event, like an illness or an operation, forces them to stop all their activity do they realize they are depressed. Others hide from it by focusing only on physical symptoms. Only when enough doctors have told them that they can't find a physical cause for their problems do they finally face the possibility of an emotional problem. And that usually ends up being depression.

Here's a short test that can help you identify where you stand in relation to depression. As you go through it, read each item carefully and put a check mark in the box that best reflects how you have been feeling during the past couple of days. If in doubt, make your best guess. If you can't decide, put your check mark in the box that reflects how you've been feeling more often than not.

Depression Test

	Seldom, if ever	Some of the time	Often, or all the time
1. I get irritable or annoyed.	☐	☐	☐
2. I feel sad.	☐	☐	☐
3. There is no pleasure in my life.	☐	☐	☐
4. I am critical of myself for my weaknesses or mistakes.	☐	☐	☐
5. My appetite has changed.	☐	☐	☐
6. I don't sleep very well.	☐	☐	☐
7. I am less interested in sex.	☐	☐	☐
8. I feel guilty.	☐	☐	☐
9. I have thoughts of killing myself.	☐	☐	☐
10. I worry about physical problems.	☐	☐	☐
11. I have trouble concentrating.	☐	☐	☐
12. Decisions are very difficult.	☐	☐	☐
13. I wish I could die.	☐	☐	☐
14. I feel I have nothing to look forward to.	☐	☐	☐
15. I feel tired all the time.	☐	☐	☐

Interpreting the Depression Test

Now that you have completed the test, count up the number of answers you have in each column. The answers in the first column have a value of zero, so they will not affect your total score. The answers in the second column are each worth one point, and the answers in the third column are each worth two points. Total the scores for each column and then add them together for your total score. The lower your score, the less depressed you are feeling, whereas the higher your score, the more severe your depression. You can evaluate your score by using the following:

Total Score	Levels of Depression
0–5	No problem with depression
6–10	Mild depression
11–15	Moderate depression
16–20	Severe depression
21–30	Extreme depression

If your score is 11 or above, you should seek some professional treatment for your depression. The higher your score, the more urgent it is for you to seek help. This is especially true if your answers to the questions would have been just the same over a period of several months.

You also need to pay close attention to questions 9 and 13, especially if either of your answers to these two questions is in the third column. These questions relate to any suicidal tendencies you may be experiencing and are serious enough that if your score was a 2 for either of these questions, it is extremely urgent that you seek professional help. If you can't do that, you need to share these thoughts and feelings with your pastor. The problem isn't just the suicidal thoughts you are identifying, but those thoughts are also primary indicators of how serious your feelings of hopelessness have become. It is this hopelessness that needs to be treated.

Also, if your answer to question 10 is in the second or third column, it might be important for you to consult with your medical doctor. Depression can cause a number of physical symptoms, but physical problems may be indicating a treatable illness that has as one of its symptoms feelings of depression.

The interplay between the physical and the emotional aspects of depression has always been confusing. Some approach depression as if the answer lies completely in medication. For some types of depression, this is and should be the major focus of treatment. For example, some depression is genetic and hereditary. When we look back at our family tree and see that one or both parents struggled with depression, and maybe their parents and siblings struggled with depression as well, we can see evidence of a biochemical foundation to this condition. This type of depression must be treated with medication, just as weak eyesight must be treated with glasses or contact lenses.

The brain chemistry does change when we are depressed, but for most of us the question is which came first—the changes in our brain chemistry or the emotional despair. Dr. Aaron Beck, one of the early theorists who advocated the treatment of depression by changing a person's Self-Talk, developed an interesting experiment. He recruited a number of people experiencing similar levels of depression and divided them into two groups. One group was treated for twelve weeks with an antidepressant medication; the other group was treated for twelve weeks with therapy focused only on their Self-Talk. This second group received no medication.

At the end of twelve weeks, the results were quite unexpected, especially in showing the significant amount of differences between the two groups. In the group receiving only the medication, approximately 20 percent showed complete recovery and almost 33 percent of the group dropped out before completing the twelve weeks. In the group working only on their Self-Talk, over 75 percent showed complete recovery and only 10 percent of the group either dropped out or failed to show any improvement. In a follow-up of the participants a year later, the gains recorded at the end of twelve weeks were maintained by both groups. Medication helped, and in some cases was absolutely necessary, but medication alone didn't help nearly as much as attitude. Attitude is everything, or at least, in the case of depression, almost everything!

Depression in the Bible

In chapter 2 we looked at Jeremiah's description of his depression in Lamentations 3:1–20. One of the descriptions the Bible uses for depression is *downcast* or *cast down*. In verse 20, after Jeremiah has recited all of the horrible things he has experienced, he finishes by saying, "My soul . . . is bowed down within me."

The root of the Hebrew word used here is the same as that used in Psalm 42:5, where the psalmist asks,

> Why are you cast down, O my soul,
> and why are you disquieted within me?

It is a refrain he picks up again in verse 11, and then again in Psalm 43:5. The root meaning of the Hebrew word is "to sink" or "to depress." In each reference, the writer is speaking about depression. And as Jeremiah does in Lamentations 3:21, the psalmist answers his own *why* question by changing his focus, his Self-Talk. He tells himself to:

> Hope in God; for I shall again praise him,
> my help and my God.
>
> Psalm 42:5

Obviously, Jeremiah and the psalmist weren't the only biblical figures who struggled with depression. King Saul suffered from a major depression for most of his adult life. His depression set in when God removed the anointing from him as God's appointed king. First Samuel 16:14 marks the beginning of Saul's depression: "Now the Spirit of the Lord departed from Saul, and an evil spirit from the Lord tormented him."

This is a difficult passage to explain. We have a hard time understanding how God could torment Saul with an "evil spirit." This phrase can also be translated "a spirit of evil" or "a spirit of affliction." Many times when we see the word *affliction* in the Old Testament, it contains the meaning of "depression." We see this, for example, in Joseph's naming his second son Ephraim, which means, "God has made me fruitful in the land of my affliction" (Gen. 41:52), or "in the land of my depression." Joseph must have experienced despair and depression, especially when he spent thirteen years in prison unjustly accused.

We can also experience depression as an attack from the enemy of our soul. In Saul's case, the passage could also mean that an oppressive evil spirit had attacked him. Obviously, there are spiritual reasons for depression. When we sin, as Saul did in being disobedient, we can experience depression. When there is sin in our lives, we certainly open ourselves to the enemy and his attacks on our heart and mind. We've already noted that the weapons of our spiritual warfare are the weapons of the mind and of our thoughts (see 2 Cor. 10:3–6).

In both Saul's and Joseph's cases, their depression is directly related to the external events going on in their lives and to their inner dialogue, or Self-Talk regarding those events. Saul is depressed because God has removed his anointing from him as king. Joseph is depressed because he has been abandoned by everyone in his life and sits unjustly accused in a prison in a strange land. We can understand their depression, for there is something specific we can point to as a major traumatic event in their lives. When we can directly connect our own feelings of depression to some hurtful, painful, unfair event in our lives, we can at least understand why we feel depressed. But depression isn't always that reasonable or logical.

Let's look at Elijah. In 1 Kings 18 we read about one of the most dramatic events in biblical history. One man, Elijah, takes on King Ahab, Queen Jezebel, and her 450 prophets of Baal. In many ways he is also taking on all of Israel, for the people have turned their backs on God and embraced the worship of Baal. All day long Elijah bravely and boldly stands alone, confronting the prophets, the people, and their false god. He challenges them to "wake him up," then chides them by laughingly saying their god must be too busy, or perhaps their god is traveling or sitting in the bathroom. "Shout louder," he tells them, "so that Baal can hear you and devour his sacrifice." But nothing happens.

Then, as evening approaches, Elijah first instructs the people to repair the altar of the Lord, then he prepares the wood and his sacrifice. Finally, in what must have appeared an absurd act, three times he soaks the sacrifice, the wood, and the altar with water. As all of Israel stands there silently watching, Elijah, with a simple prayer of faith, calls down the fire from heaven that not only devours the sacrifice but licks up the water in the trench as well! It is a day of victory for Elijah and the one true God. As an encore, Elijah then prays for rain to end a three-year drought, and when his servant sees a "cloud like a man's hand . . . rising out of the sea," Elijah tells King Ahab to head for home before the downpour begins.

It seems reasonable to believe that after such a great victory over the false prophets, Elijah would have been even more confident in the Lord's power and protection. But a message from Queen Jezebel saying that she will have his life within twenty-four hours as revenge sends Elijah running. First, he runs from Mount Carmel, way up in the northwest corner of Israel, all the way to Beersheba, as far south as one could go and still be in Judah. But that isn't far enough for Elijah. Leaving his servant there, he continues to run south for another full day.

There, deeply tired and depressed, he collapses under a broom tree and prays "that he might die" (1 Kings 19:4 TLB). "'I've had enough,' he tells the Lord. 'Take away my life. I've got to die sometime, and it might as well be now.'" Elijah has just experienced his two greatest spiritual victories, and immediately after them, he is so depressed he wants to die. That's an example of an irrational depression. To the outside observer, what Elijah is experiencing just doesn't make sense. We can understand the depression experienced by King Saul, Joseph, or even Jeremiah, but not Elijah. Perhaps that is why what Elijah is experiencing can give us important insight into some of the more troubling parts of our own struggles with depression—depression that comes when on the surface all seems to be going well.

Elijah's Self-Talk

What sets off the feelings of despair and fear in Elijah? We can easily see in Scripture that Queen Jezebel has threatened his life, but to all appearances that threat is nothing compared to the risk he has just taken in challenging the prophets of Baal. Reason would say, "If God could provide such a dramatic victory over Ahab, Jezebel, and the 450 false prophets, why would God abandon Elijah now?"

But reason isn't a part of Elijah's depression. Perhaps it is the brashness of Jezebel's message; or it is the natural letdown that follows an exhausting victory; or perhaps it is Elijah's own feelings of insecurity in that perhaps God doesn't need him any longer—we can't be certain of what triggers the fear in Elijah. But once triggered, we can easily identify some of the patterns of Elijah's Self-Talk, that inner dialogue that goes on within the privacy of his own thoughts. Thoughts like:

What if Jezebel means it? After all, her messenger found me.

What if God is finished with me?

Maybe I don't really matter that much to God.

After all, who am I really in God's eyes—I'm just a worm!

I better take care of myself.

With thoughts like these, Elijah sets in motion a cycle of negative Self-Talk that leads him into the depths of depression, despair, and hopelessness. We who are standing outside the circumstances can see how irrational and untrue these statements are that he is choosing to believe. But if we had been in Elijah's shoes, we would have probably thought similar things, felt the same way, and done the same thing. That's the way we sinful human beings seem to work when we try to figure it out on our own.

Patterns of Distorted Self-Talk

Dr. Aaron Beck has identified six patterns of distortion that all of us use at some time or other in our Self-Talk.[2] These systematic errors in our thinking are at the root of our depression. In spite of the evidence, or even of the reasonable arguments that friends and loved ones use to try to help us overcome our depression, these six patterns help to maintain our negative pattern of thinking.

114

1. *Arbitrary inference.* This error in our Self-Talk refers to our tendency to draw conclusions in the absence of any evidence. We will draw our conclusion even when all the evidence points to the opposite. Elijah uses this faulty process when he assumes that Jezebel can actually follow through on her threat to kill him and that God is unable to protect him. Elijah believes this despite all the overwhelming evidence he has just experienced showing God's power and protection.

Often, our family of origin has played a role in setting this pattern in motion. We may have a graduate degree and be very competent in our work as well as in our life. But because a parent made a habit of calling us stupid, we are always fighting the thought "I'm stupid." In some ways, we really believe we are stupid in spite of the evidence that says our intelligence is way above average.

2. *Selective abstraction.* This pattern will take a small detail out of context and focus only on that one detail, ignoring other more powerful and important information. Elijah also uses this pattern. When he complains to God that he is the only one left in all of Israel who is faithful to God, he has just experienced his aloneness in facing the prophets of Baal. He takes that experience and makes an absolute out of it. But God has to remind him that there are still seven thousand others in Israel who are faithful.

We see selective abstraction at work when we hear a beautiful woman zero in on one flaw she sees in her skin or who believes she is ugly because she has a slightly crooked place on her nose. Or we hear the housewife who says her house is filthy because she didn't finish cleaning the baseboards. All the evidence says her house is clean, but to her it is filthy.

3. *Overgeneralization.* This describes our tendency to take several isolated incidents and then believe that these constitute a general pattern. An example would be someone who grew up in

115

an abusive home. Several times the father became physically abusive, and the physical abuse always followed verbal abuse. Now, whenever anyone shouts at that person, he or she is convinced that physical hurt will follow, even though there are countless examples of his or her being shouted at and suffering no physical abuse.

4. *Magnification and minimization.* I call this "the M & M disease."[3] In this pattern we minimize a broad range of evidence and then blow out of proportion one aspect of an event. For example, Mary has spent all morning cleaning the house, but before she can finish the last detail a friend stops by. Mary is flustered, embarrassed, and very sincere as she apologizes for her "messy house." No one but Mary would notice the final detail of her housecleaning routine; but because it isn't finished, she minimizes what is done and magnifies what isn't done.

Or take Tom, who used to make beautiful pieces of furniture out of wood. Friends offered to pay him to make them something. He not only refused, but he now has quit making things for himself, for every time he looked at something he had made, all he could see was some minor flaw. In his eyes, that flaw spoiled the whole piece of furniture for him.

5. *Personalization.* Some of us, either through personality or family training, have a tendency to relate all kinds of external events to ourselves, even when we know there is no basis whatever for such a relationship. Jeremiah did this in Lamentations 3. Much of his despair came from his feeling that God had abandoned *him* when the nation of Judah fell. It was his fault. He didn't preach clearly enough or often enough or strongly enough. Somehow he had let God down. And in the process of personalizing, Jeremiah forgot that it was the people who had abandoned God.

6. *Absolutistic, dichotomous thinking.* This pattern is at the root of perfectionism, and perfectionism is a guaranteed path to

depression. In this pattern we tend to divide the world into one of two opposite categories: for example, perfect or worthless, spotless or filthy, good or bad, saint or sinner. In depression, our inner dialogue, our Self-Talk, will take on this dichotomy, and we apply the awful, hopeless, helpless part to ourselves and can only attribute positive action and power to someone else. Our dichotomous thinking paralyzes us in our helplessness and then feeds right into depression.

We will take these six ways of distorting our Self-Talk and apply them in our evaluation of ourselves, of our world, of others, and even of God. I've talked with people who are depressed and tried to show them some of God's promises to those who are "cast down." But their distorted thinking about God can only see him as a punishing figure—"God is punishing me for something I did."

Perhaps you have tried to point out areas of hope to a depressed loved one only to have the loved one say time after time, "Yes, but . . ." When we understand how these distortions affect our Self-Talk, we can see why it is so difficult to break out of depression. When depressed, our thoughts are dominated by an overwhelming negativity. Then, because we use arbitrary inference or some other distorted pattern, we focus only on those negative events and perceptions that support our negativity. We minimize everything else. As we believe the worst, things will often actually get worse, which only further reinforces our depression and hopelessness.

When we look to our past, we see only our failures and things that make us feel guilty. When we look to our future, we see only emptiness and hopelessness. "Nothing will ever change!" we tell ourselves. When we look at our present, we see only those negative, oppressive things that reinforce all the horrible thoughts we already believe to be true. In Romans 7 Paul struggles with this sense of being trapped. It's no wonder that he finally cries out,

"Wretched man that I am! Who will deliver me from this body of death?" (Rom. 7:24).

Breaking Depression with Self-Talk

In looking at Elijah's experience, we can identify six things we can do to break the cycle of depression in our lives. When we are depressed, everything within us will work to keep us from taking any of these steps. But if we can, with God's help, take one small step in the direction of doing step one, we may be able to start up a different cycle in our Self-Talk—one that will cause us to find even the smallest ray of hope.

1. Do Something

Do something, no matter how small a step it is. Do anything! Well, almost anything. It is the willful choice to act that breaks through our sense of helplessness. I remember one woman who had been depressed for some time and nothing seemed to help her break the cycle. Everything I suggested was met with either a "Yes, but . . ." or was simply ignored. Finally I got her attention. At the end of one session I told her that her assignment for the week was to go home and pick a day that week in which she was "going to enjoy being depressed." Her instructions were to not even get dressed that day, but to simply stay in bed all day and "enjoy being depressed." She could lie in her bed and watch anything on TV she wanted to watch, eat anything she wanted to eat. The only catch was that she was to do it intentionally and to try to enjoy doing it. At first she thought I was crazy, but then she thought awhile and picked a day when she didn't have to carpool.

At our next meeting she described the surprise and shock on her daughter's face when she came home from school and found her still in bed in her pajamas eating potato chips and watching TV. But it worked! Because she did it intentionally—that means she chose to do it—she "did something." That marked the beginning of the end of her struggle with depression.

Elijah runs for his life. He runs all across Israel and across Judah. When he stops running, God tells him to run some more. In fact, God sends him to Mount Sinai, which is all the way to the bottom of the Sinai Peninsula—a journey of forty days and nights through the desert. Elijah is depressed. God adds a new assignment that probably doesn't make sense to Elijah, but he does it. He does something. And his depression is on its way out.

What can you do? It really doesn't matter too much as long as you choose to do something. Perhaps you decide to get up an hour earlier and get dressed right away. Or you decide to fix breakfast for the family, something you haven't done since you've been depressed. The decision to do something gives you a sense of being back in control, even if it is only something small. When God tells Elijah to keep going, God is back in control of Elijah's life. Jezebel no longer dictates what he is going to do—God does and Elijah agrees!

2. Take Care of Yourself

When we are depressed we often stop taking care of ourselves. For some of us, depression is the result of becoming burned out from taking care of everyone else but ourselves. Notice what God does for Elijah when he wants to die there under the broom tree (see 1 Kings 19:5). After allowing Elijah to sleep, an angel awakens him and says, "Get up and eat." After Elijah has eaten, God lets him sleep some more before feeding him again and sending him on his way.

Taking care of yourself when you are depressed can mean a number of things. For example, it may mean that you make an appointment to see your physician and get a full medical checkup.

That satisfies both steps one and two—you're doing something and taking care of yourself. Or it may mean that you change the way you eat and start eating good, healthy meals. For someone else it might mean asking a husband to take the kids for an evening so she can soak in a hot bath and relax for a couple of hours. You know what it is you wish you could do. If it is a good thing to do, do it and give yourself permission to enjoy it.

Sometimes, when we are depressed, taking care of ourselves is the hardest thing we can do. We are so down on ourselves that the thought of doing something nice fills us with added guilt. But spend some time and meditate on God's attitude toward Elijah when he is depressed. God doesn't reprimand him. In fact, God never does do that to Elijah. Instead, God takes care of his prophet. He feeds him, lets him sleep, and then reminds Elijah of his character and power. God gives Elijah exactly what he needs, and God will do that for you as well. Let him take care of you, but that means also that *you* have to take care of you.

3. Challenge the Distortions in Your Self-Talk

The third thing God does with Elijah is challenge the distortions in his thinking. When Elijah arrives at Mount Sinai, he goes into a cave and rests. Then God comes, and again, instead of reprimanding Elijah, he asks him a simple question: "What are you doing here, Elijah?" (1 Kings 19:13).

Look at Elijah's answer:

> I have been very zealous for the LORD, the God of hosts; for the people of Israel have forsaken thy covenant, thrown down thy altars, and slain thy prophets with the sword, and I, even I only, am left; and they seek my life, to take it away.
>
> 1 Kings 19:14

Look at the distortions. In chapter 18 the people rebuilt the altar of God and cried out, "The LORD, he is God!" Then they literally destroyed the false prophets of Baal. Has Elijah forgotten all of that? Apparently so. Does God chastise him for his distorted perception? Not according to Scripture. Instead, God goes beyond the symptoms and the distortions and gets right to the heart of the matter. For some reason, Elijah has forgotten that God is the all-powerful Yahweh, so God puts on an incredible display of his power for Elijah.

First, God sends a powerful wind that tears the mountains apart. Then he sends an earthquake, followed by a fire. God isn't in those powerful events; he just sends them for Elijah's benefit. Finally, God speaks to Elijah in a gentle voice, asking him the same question he asked before. What Elijah needs to know is not that God is more powerful than anything Elijah has experienced. He has already seen that on Mount Carmel. The question that haunts Elijah in the depths of his despair is, "But is God still interested in the man Elijah?" The gentle whisper speaks directly to Elijah's heart and his need to see this part of God's character. And God lovingly reveals it to him.

When you start challenging the distortions in your Self-Talk, get ready for some new experiences and some new understandings of what the truth really can be for you. Open yourself to seeing parts of God which you have, in your distorted perceptions, struggled against believing could possibly exist. God wants to show himself to each of us, and he especially wants us to see and experience those parts of him that seem too good to be true.

4. Refocus

Much of what God does there on Mount Sinai with Elijah is to refocus Elijah's perception of God. Perhaps Elijah has distorted his perception of God and believes that God only cares about the big things, like getting rid of the prophets of Baal, but that God doesn't really care about the little things, like taking care of Elijah and protecting him from Jezebel.

In chapter 2 we talked about the importance of our perceived center of control. Elijah's perceptions need to be corrected, and when we are depressed our perceptions usually need to be corrected as well. God is still in control, even though Elijah isn't so certain of that when he runs. And even in the midst of our deepest despair, God is still in control and nothing escapes his loving concern.

Not only does Elijah need to refocus and correct his perception of God, he needs to refocus his anger. Jezebel is the proper target for his anger; but when he gives in to his fear, he is afraid to be angry with her. I've found that people who are depressed usually have a problem with anger. It isn't that they aren't angry, it is that the anger is all directed at the self rather than at the one who is really deserving of their anger. Elijah has good reason to be angry with Jezebel. But he gives in to his fear instead. Where is his anger directed? Probably at himself, because he feels so powerless to stand up against her, and at God, because he doesn't believe God will or can protect him. Elijah is angry with everyone and everything but the real source of his problem—Jezebel.

Where's your anger directed? At yourself mostly? Try refocusing your anger where it really belongs and see what that does to the feelings of depression and helplessness. It isn't easy to do when you're depressed, but it will change the way you're feeling.

5. Limit the Depressive Symptoms

As you read through 1 Kings 19, it is interesting to note that God doesn't enter into a discussion with Elijah about the cause of his depression. Twice God asks him, "Why are you here, Elijah?" but neither time does God ask Elijah to elaborate or explain, and neither time does God offer any sympathy for what Elijah is saying. Instead, God does two things. He reveals more of himself to Elijah, and he gives Elijah something to do.

In a way, this step is an extension of the last step, where we refocus our attention. God gives Elijah something that needs to be done that will keep him busy with the work of ministry. He is to anoint Hazael king over Aram, and he is to anoint Elisha as his assistant and companion.

Here's a way to experience what God was doing with Elijah. When you finish this paragraph, stop reading and notice any feelings you might have of depression. After you have noted how you feel, pick up an object in your room and begin to examine it. Notice every detail you can about that object from as many different angles as possible. When you have finished examining the object, stop again and note how you are feeling. Most people feel better after examining the object than they did before. The reason is that they have focused on something outside themselves, on something other than how they are feeling.

It is important to limit the symptoms you are experiencing if you are depressed. That doesn't mean you deny the symptoms; you simply set limits on how long you will focus on those feelings. For example, if you feel like crying and sometimes wonder if you can stop, set a time limit on how long you will cry. Give yourself five minutes to cry, and at the end of the five minutes, stop. If you find yourself ruminating about some of the hurts or losses you have experienced, set a time when you will sit down and write out some of those feelings. Then don't allow yourself to linger with those feelings at other times. Finding the balance between allowing yourself to experience the hurt, the loss, and the sadness, yet not allowing yourself to be swallowed up by those feelings is what is meant by this step of limiting the symptoms.

6. *Break the Pattern of Isolation*

When we are depressed, our despair often drives us into isolation. We cut off relationships with the very people who care for us and want to stand with us as we work through the pain. It seems like it's us against the world, and we're losing. When Elijah is depressed under the broom tree, he is alone. He has left his servant in Beersheba and gone on by himself. It's almost part of the very nature of depression—we want to be alone with our pain. Yet the worst thing we can do is be alone.

Both times Elijah answers God's question, Elijah points out that he is the only one left who is faithful to the Lord. He is standing alone against the world. God's solution to Elijah's isolating himself is to tell him to anoint Elisha to succeed him as prophet and to let Elisha spend time with him. When Elijah anoints Elisha, Elisha asks Elijah to wait while he says good-bye to his parents. Elijah is still resisting having someone spend time with him. Apparently he is still more comfortable operating in isolation, so he says to Elisha, "Go on back! Why all the excitement?" (1 Kings 19:20 TLB). It is as if he is saying, "No rush—you don't need to spend time with me." But Elisha wants to be with Elijah, so after offering his sacrifice and saying good-bye, he catches up with Elijah and serves as his assistant.

Notice, too, the little aside God makes to Elijah back on Mount Sinai. After God has finished with his instructions for Elijah, he adds, "And incidentally, there are 7,000 men in Israel who have never bowed to Baal nor kissed him!" (v. 18 TLB). "Elijah," God says, "you're not alone!"

And neither are we. It's interesting that people who report that they are lonely have been found to have more people contact than those who are not bothered by loneliness. We often feel lonely because in some way we want to do it by ourselves. Loneliness is an attitude, just as depression can be an attitude. The battle against both begins in our minds, in our Self-Talk.

Questions for Personal Growth and Discussion

1. Look at how you did on the Depression Test. What factors contribute to your score?

2. What are some of the patterns of thought distortion you use most often? How does your pattern of thought distortion affect your emotions?

3. Which step in breaking the pattern of depression is most difficult for you? Which is easiest? Why?

SEVEN

Self-Talk and Guilt

No condemnation now hangs over the head of those who are
"in" Christ Jesus.

Romans 8:1 PHILLIPS

Several years ago I traveled and led seminars with a group of men, one of whom had a line he used with the waitress when we were eating. Near the end of the meal, when she came around to ask about dessert, he would ask, "Do you have any scruples?" And most of the waitresses weren't quite sure what scruples were, so they'd give some evasive answer. Then he would ask her to check with the cook or the manager. A little later, she'd come back with a red face and a funny smile, knowing he'd set her up. Usually, someone in the kitchen knew that a scruple had something to do with moral or ethical standards.

John Powell in his book *Why Am I Afraid to Love?* points out that *scruple* is derived from the Latin word for a small, sharp stone. Those small stones apparently were used as measures of weight and still are by pharmacists. Powell relates scruples to guilt and says that "when by accident a small pebble gets lodged inside one of our shoes, as we walk along we feel the intermittent stabs of pain. So the scrupulous person, as he walks through life, feels the intermittent agonies of his imagined guilt." Scruples give us something to feel guilty about.

Guilt is often attached to feelings of anger and depression and always relates to the past. We can't feel guilty about the future—that just doesn't make sense. Guilt takes us away from the present, back into the past, in an attempt to reform the past. Dr. Thomas Oden, author of *Structure of Awareness,* describes this on a time line that looks like this:

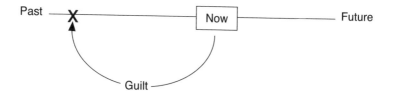

We go back in our memories to the past in an effort to remake that past so we won't feel as guilty. We want to get rid of that stone in our shoe. But experience is all of one piece. We can't separate any past event from our experience—it all stays there. So instead we try to reshape our memory of that event so that we come out looking better.

We really don't have to look very far to see how we developed the ability to feel guilty in our Self-Talk. Parents are great teachers of guilt. They didn't teach us how to feel guilty when they spanked us. That punishment effectively eliminated the need for feeling guilty—we hurt instead. But when our parents gave us one of those silent looks across the room that said, "If you don't straighten up, you're going to get it at home!" we experienced feelings of guilt.

Our spouses and children continue the job of making us feel guilty. Teachers and preachers also know how to stimulate feelings of guilt. I had a first-grade teacher who did a masterful job with me. She was always telling me I wasn't working up to my potential. Her tone of voice made it sound as though that were some awful kind of behavior, so I felt guilty.

Friends, employers, fellow employees—the list of guilt producers is endless. It seems as if people exist for the purpose of making others feel guilty.

Now the problem is complicated by our Self-Talk. Our memory takes us back to a guilt-producing experience. Then we remember other events further back in our memory that only serve to substantiate the feelings of guilt we are struggling with in our Self-Talk. This can be shown on the time line as follows:

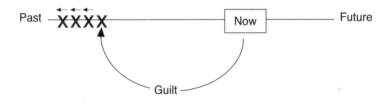

Take the example of my not working up to my potential. When the teacher told me that, my Self-Talk agreed with her and quickly went back to other examples that proved I didn't work up to my potential. My parents jumped on the bandwagon, and when my grades were not high enough, they said, "You're not working up to your potential." So then my Self-Talk would look at my grades and I would feel guilty. My Self-Talk could also look back to other test scores and other events related to the experience of being told I wasn't working up to my potential. And my guilt was validated. "I'm guilty!" And by my Self-Talk I added another small, sharp stone to the ones in my shoe.

Now some guilt is valid. Obviously, when we have done something that is clearly wrong, the guilt we feel is correct and serves to push us to correct the wrong. This is what Paul calls a "godly grief" in 2 Corinthians 7:9–10:

> I rejoice, not because you were grieved, but because you were grieved into repenting; for you felt a godly grief, so that you suffered no loss through us. For godly grief produces a repentance that leads to salvation and brings no regret, but worldly grief produces death.

The guilt we are dealing with in this chapter is neurotic guilt, or false guilt. It is the kind of guilt that locks us out of the present and keeps us in the past. And every example of guilt contains a should or shouldn't.

I shouldn't have done that!

I should have done that instead!

So what do you do? You try harder! At least that's what you do at first. If you're feeling guilty because your husband is angry at you for not having dinner on the table when he gets home, you try harder to meet his expectations. But then he's a few minutes early, and you've blown it again. But you keep on trying harder.

Or you blow up at him and try to set up some standards for him to meet. "If you want dinner on the table when you come home, then you'd better be home at the same time every night, and you'd better help out more around the house so I have the time to get dinner ready, and . . ."

But every time you set up a new standard that arises out of guilt, it just gives you something more to feel guilty about. And the harder you try, the more you find that you fail. I think that's what sin is.

Paul wrestles with this in Romans 7. Paul has been trying harder and harder to meet the demands of the law. He sets up new and tighter standards for himself and finds that all he is doing is frustrating himself and creating more guilt. The experience he describes in this chapter is evidence of the tyranny of the shoulds!

We can sum up Paul's struggle in Romans 7 in the following way: "The things that I should do, I don't do. And the things that I shouldn't do, I do! Oh, wretched man that I am! Who will break this pattern?"

He knows what he wants to do, but he doesn't do it. And he knows what not to do, but he finds himself doing it. As a result, he is miserably depressed! Paul has gone back in his memories to experiences that trigger feelings of guilt. These memories, in turn, trigger other feelings of guilt. Then Paul comes back into the now, not only with his feelings of guilt but also with new standards and shoulds that he has set for himself. And these new standards and shoulds only give him something new to feel guilty over. And the more he tries to change (the more he tries to meet these new standards), the guiltier he feels. No wonder he ends up depressed! Using the time line, we can illustrate Paul's struggle like this:

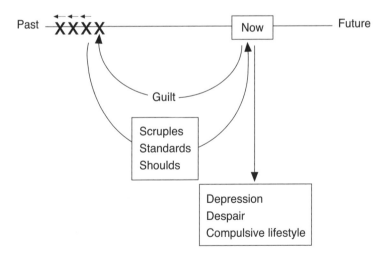

The solution to Paul's struggle in Romans 7 is found in the opening verse of the next chapter, where he says, "There is therefore now no condemnation for those who are in Christ Jesus." Nothing can condemn Paul! There is nothing Paul can do or not do that will condemn him. There are therefore now no shoulds!

That Paul learned this lesson is seen in his first letter to the Corinthians. Twice he makes the point that "all things are lawful for me" (1 Cor. 6:12). There are no shoulds in Paul's life. And the result is that now he is able to do the things he wants to do. He is able to avoid doing those things he doesn't want to do. And the same will work for you.

But note, those verses are not just blanket statements. He does list some qualifiers. "'All things are lawful for me,' but not all things are helpful. 'All things are lawful for me,' but I will not be enslaved by anything." And again, in chapter 10, verse 23, he adds, "'All things are lawful,' but not all things build up." The qualifiers he adds are good common sense, not demands. The point remains the same: All things are lawful, so remove the demands on yourself!

If we don't remove the demands or shoulds we place on ourselves, one of two things will occur. We've already seen that these demands will create guilt. The other thing that occurs is that we become paralyzed and depressed. Our guilt will make us angry with ourselves, and that is one of the major causes of depression.

Notice how it builds. You're sitting in the office after your friend and co-worker has told you the details about his promotion and raise. After he leaves, you sit there angry at yourself. Your Self-Talk sounds something like this:

I should have worked harder for that promotion.

I'm as good a worker as he is. They should've considered me more seriously.

How awful. I'll never get anyplace in this company.

I've got to work harder.

Better look busy—there's the boss.

I'll show them how good I am.

Dummy! You should have known this would happen. Now what are you going to do?

Maybe I'd better get my resumé out.

Nuts, I'm going home early.

And as long as you grovel in that kind of Self-Talk, you'll either sit there immobilized or you'll go home and get depressed because you're so angry at yourself.

Even Ziggy, the little cartoon character, knows this. One Sunday, after shoulding himself all over the house and all over the comic page, he sprawls out in his easy chair. As he sits there, he says to himself, "I should stop 'shoulding' myself." Until he stops shoulding

himself, he'll sit there paralyzed by his guilt and his shoulds. Just like Paul in Romans 7, he's only a short step away from despair.

When you go back into the past to try to re-form some event that triggers your guilt, you are usually dealing with a lot of anger directed at yourself. And sometimes your guilt, your anger at yourself, and your anger at others and God get all tangled up. Elijah has that kind of experience when he challenges the prophets of Baal to a showdown on Mount Carmel. He invites the 450 prophets of Baal and the 400 prophets of Asherah to meet him and find out which God is real. In 1 Kings 18 Elijah has a field day. He taunts the prophets, telling them that perhaps their god is asleep or on a journey. Then Elijah has his chance. He sets up the altar, pours water all over it, then prays a short, simple prayer. "Then the fire of the LORD fell, and consumed the burnt offering, and the wood, and the stones, and the dust, and licked up the water that was in the trench" (v. 38). After that, Elijah orders all the false prophets to be killed. What a moment of victory!

But in 1 Kings 19 Jezebel sends a message to Elijah, telling him she is going to kill him that day. And Elijah flees in fear. After running for the whole day, he collapses under a broom tree and asks that he might die. He's filled with despair. Why? Perhaps his Self-Talk goes something like this: "Why didn't I take care of Jezebel when I took care of all those false prophets? Why didn't I think of that? She's the problem, and dumb me, I overlooked it. Now look at the mess I'm in."

Then he may also be angry with God: "God, you should've taken care of her. After all, look at all I did for you!"

And then he probably feels guilty for talking to God like that. So his guilt, his anger, and his self-reproach all add up to a total feeling of despair and the desire only to die.

Jonah does the same thing. He fights against God's direction to go to Nineveh. Then, after three days' consideration in the belly of a great fish, he reluctantly goes and proclaims the message God gave him. The king of Nineveh hears the message, repents, and orders the whole city to repent. In chapter 4 we read that "it displeased Jonah exceedingly, and he was angry" (v. 1). His anger is directed at God for asking him to preach a message of repentance to one of Israel's enemies. But he must also be struggling with feelings of guilt and self-directed anger, for in verse 3, he pleads, "Therefore now, O LORD, take my life from me, I beseech thee, for it is better for me to die than to live."

Poor Jonah. He is immersed in self-pity. Perhaps he is angry at God and himself for what has happened. After all, what will they say back home? He is caught in a shoulding cycle that is directed at God and himself. The result is despair.

The cycle of false guilt traps you in attempts to reshape the past and then to come back into the present with an expanded set of shoulds, standards, and scruples. The cycle leads to a lifestyle that is prone to depression and despair. And that pattern, if left unchecked, can lead to illness and even death.

Now maybe you're feeling that you should really do something about your guilt and anger. *That* will only lead you to more guilt and anger. What you need to do is something that breaks the entire cycle.

First, you must recognize the source of your false guilt. It is in your mind—your Self-Talk. If the source is in your Self-Talk, the solution lies there as well.

The Solution

David helps us understand the solution to the problem of guilt and self-directed anger. When he stays home from the battle and in his boredom has an affair with Bathsheba, David not only violates another man's wife, he commits murder as well. For some time after that event, he carefully controls both his anger at himself and his very valid feelings of guilt. Then the prophet Nathan comes along with a parable that penetrates deep within David to the root of his guilt and anger (see 2 Sam. 12:1–14).

Later, after the confrontation with his own sinfulness, David writes Psalm 51 and shows us how he dealt with his guilt. He breaks away from the shoulds that would only lead to more guilt and anger and, instead, gets right to the heart of the matter. That is repentance and forgiveness.

He begins by saying,

> Have mercy on me, O God,
>> according to thy steadfast love;
> according to thy abundant mercy
>> blot out my transgressions.
> Wash me thoroughly from my iniquity,
>> and cleanse me from my sin!
>>>>> verses 1–2

Notice the guilt he experiences:

> For I know my transgressions,
>> and my sin is ever before me.
> Against thee, thee only, have I sinned,
>> and done that which is evil in thy sight.
>>>>> verses 3–4

A little later in the psalm he asks,

> Fill me with joy and gladness;
>> let the bones which thou hast broken rejoice. . . .
> Create in me a clean heart, O God,
>> and put a new and right spirit within me.
> Cast me not away from thy presence,
>> and take not thy holy Spirit from me.

136

> Restore to me the joy of thy salvation,
> and uphold me with a willing spirit.
>
> verses 8, 10–12

David is asking for forgiveness. And only forgiveness can resolve the downward cycle of guilt—both valid and false.

But our tendency, remember, is to try a little harder. "Give me a little more time, and I'll prove what a good person I am," we plead. But time and trying will not break the cycle.

Jesus illustrates this in a parable in Matthew 18:23–35. In the context of Peter's question about forgiveness, Jesus says:

> The Kingdom of Heaven can be compared to a king who decided to bring his accounts up to date. In the process, one of his debtors was brought in who owed him $10,000,000! He couldn't pay, so the king ordered him sold for the debt, also his wife and children and everything he had.
>
> But the man fell down before the king, his face in the dust, and said, "Oh, sir, be patient with me and I will pay it all."
>
> verses 23–26 TLB

How absurd! Yet how like us. He owes his master ten million dollars, and he asks for a little more time. Perhaps he is thinking, "I'll try a little harder! I should have written him a letter explaining my situation." He owes a debt. He is guilty. And all he can do is ask for more time in which to try harder! "Then the king was filled with pity for him and released him and *forgave his debt*" (v. 27 TLB, italics added).

Incredible! If that had been me, I'd have been a new man. But look at him:

> But when the man left the king, he went to a man who owed him $2,000 and grabbed him by the throat and demanded instant payment.
>
> verse 28 TLB

This fellow has standards, let me tell you! He's got scruples! He has higher standards than the king.

> The man fell down before him and begged him to give him a little time. "Be patient and I will pay it," he pled.
>
> verse 29 TLB

Now you'd think a little red light would go on in that man's head, reminding him that he just said the same thing to the king. But this man is going to stick to his standards. After all, if a debt is owed, it *should* be paid. It doesn't matter what the king does. That's the way things *should* be!

> But his creditor wouldn't wait. He had the man arrested and jailed until the debt would be paid in full.
>
> Then the man's friends went to the king and told him what had happened. And the king called before him the man he had forgiven and said, "You evil-hearted wretch! Here I forgave you all that tremendous debt, just because you asked me to—shouldn't you have mercy on others, just as I had mercy on you?"
>
> Then the angry king sent the man to the torture chamber until he had paid every last penny due.
>
> verses 31–34 TLB

I think what the king is saying to this man is something like, "Don't you understand what I forgave you for? Don't you feel the extent of that forgiveness?" Apparently not, for the man acts as one who still owes a huge debt. He is walking around acting like someone who is still ten million dollars in the red. That's just like our walking around with false guilt! We've been forgiven! The debt has been erased.

Jesus finishes the parable with the admonition, "So shall my heavenly Father do to you if you refuse to truly forgive your brothers" (v. 35 TLB). And I believe we can add to that the need to forgive ourselves.

There was a man in my office recently who said, "I can't forgive myself because I can't forget!" That's setting up a bind that's hopeless because he can never forget. He can't erase that line that extends into the past. He can only forgive. That man's Self-Talk determines his problem. Because he believes he cannot experience forgiveness because he cannot forget, he will not experience forgiveness. What a difference words would make if he could change his Self-Talk to say, "I cannot forget, but I can experience forgiveness!"

Self-Talk can be an accuser or it can glory in forgiveness, as David does in Psalm 103. You can let your thoughts run wild with guilt and anger, or you can capture every thought and bring it under the umbrella of forgiveness. Destroy the shoulds, the hopeless standards, the small, sharp stones. In their place put forgiveness, for only forgiveness can cancel out the debt of guilt and anger.

What kind of Self-Talk is blocking your ability to forgive yourself? Where is your Self-Talk telling you to "try harder"? Make a list of those statements, and then with a bold black marker, write across that list *"FORGIVEN!"*

Questions for Personal Growth and Discussion

1. Who were some of your "guilt" teachers?

2. Think of some situations in which you tried to resolve guilt by "trying harder." Describe what happened.

3. Where are you still having difficulty in experiencing forgiveness? In being forgiving?

EIGHT

Self-Talk, Worry, and Anxiety

Don't worry about anything.

Philippians 4:6 TLB

What do you worry about? Money? Kids? Parents? Your health or sight? The future? Job security? Do you sometimes worry about not having anything to worry about? Or maybe you are not the one in your family who worries—you leave it all to your spouse.

Someone defined worry as "stewing without doing." That's a good definition because there is really nothing you can do about your worries since they are oriented to the future. And besides, almost everything we worry about is uncontrollable or, at least, improbable.

Since the things we worry about usually do not come to pass, our tendency to think irrationally leads us to believe that somehow through our worrying we prevent those events from happening.

And that only feeds our fears about what "might" happen, especially if we were to stop worrying. We really do worry about not having something to worry about.

Worry tends to paralyze us. We feel helpless, frustrated, unable to counteract some uncontrollable event. In looking up *worry* in the dictionary, I found that it comes from an old English word that means "to strangle, or choke." Perhaps that's how the word *worry* got attached to this feeling of helplessness. When we worry, we are strangling or choking our emotions, blocking any flow of creative energy potential in our lives.

Anxiety is similar to worry, except that anxiety does not have a specific object. It is undifferentiated. For example, we sometimes see Linus, in the Peanuts comic strip, wandering around as though he is lost. He's restless. He's experiencing anxiety. As he aimlessly moves from scene to scene with a blank look on his face, he suddenly becomes aware of why he is anxious. His blanket is missing! With that discovery, his anxiety becomes worry. His fears now have an object. So he worries about the fate of his blanket until it is recovered.

One of the difficulties we have with many of our worries is separating worry from genuine concern. We often defend our tendency to worry as being a form of caring. We care so much about our kids that it's just natural to worry about them. (Maybe that's why women tend to be the worriers, because their role is often defined as one of caring.)

But caring and concern slip very easily into worry and anxiety. The line that separates them is often difficult to define. Concern can be defined as a feeling that motivates us to action. Worry, on the other hand, paralyzes us. Concern focuses on controllable behavior and events; worry focuses on events and behavior that are beyond our control.

Worry is really an attempt to control the future. Just as guilt is an attempt to reshape the past, worry is our godlike push into the future, attempting to shape it the way we want. Of course, it is just as impossible for us to control the future as it is to reshape the past. But we persist in the attempt.

In the last chapter we drew a time line and showed how guilt related to the past and affected the present. We can complete that time line now by extending the arrow into the future in the form of worry and anxiety. You can see this on the time line below:

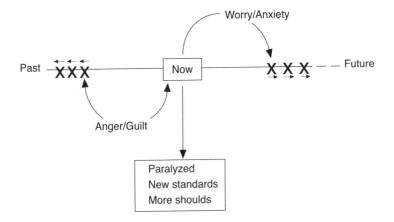

Of course, sometimes our feelings get confused. We may attach worry to events in the past. Or we try to feel guilt over some possible event in the future. The result of this confusion is anxiety—those undifferentiated fears. Anxiety intensifies unless we sort out our feelings and attach the right feeling to the right time period.

We saw in the chapter on guilt how those out-of-control feelings come back into the present, causing us to create new and higher standards of behavior. We become more scrupulous and add to our list of shoulds. Then we take these thoughts and extend them into the future, worrying over the possibility of violating these standards, scruples, or shoulds. In the process, we get so wrapped up in the past and the future that we end up paralyzed in the present.

For example, you're worried about finding a job. In your Self-Talk, you say something like this:

What if I can't find a job?

What if I use up my savings?

I must find something for a job!

It isn't fair that I lost my job!

I've got to work!

What your worried Self-Talk is doing is raising your need for a job to an absolute. "I *must* find a job!" You will accept no other alternatives! You get so caught up in your worries that you end up trapped in the present. You can barely drag yourself out of the house to find a job.

Or perhaps you worry about having enough money. Your worried Self-Talk sounds like:

What if I can't pay all my bills?

What if I get sick and can't work?

Inflation is awful! It eats up all my money!

I must get a better paying job to build up my savings!

What if I have an emergency?

What if they raise my rent? How will I afford it?

In your mind, you have created an absolute by demanding that you *must* have your financial affairs ordered in a certain way. By raising those standards to an absolute, you have insured that you have something to worry about. But in the process, you have also locked yourself into a way of thinking that limits your options. By limiting your options, you become immobilized. You can't do any creative planning because you're too busy worrying.

Sometimes our worries and anxiety lead to the development of compulsive behavior and to phobias. What if a germ gets on your hand and makes you sick? So you compulsively wash your hands. What if you run out of money? So you compulsively think you are broke if your checkbook balance falls below $500 or if you have to take some money out of your savings. What if you stand up on top of a tall building and a strong wind comes along that might blow you off? So you develop acrophobia, a fear of heights. What if you leave the house and someone or something attacks you? So you develop agoraphobia, the fear of going outside. The list of examples can go on and on, always with the result that you are immobilized in the present.

Worry can also lead to self-deception. Sometimes when I get worried about having enough money, I don't keep a balance in my checkbook. Crazy! But I can sit at my desk and look at that checkbook and the calculator and just sit! I don't want to know my balance. Maybe it's because someone once told me that what I don't know won't hurt me. But it's usually because my fear of not having enough money in that account—my worry—paralyzes me. My Self-Talk says, "I can't stand to figure out the balance! What if I don't have enough? How awful that would be!" So my ignorance is bliss, until the overdraft notice comes from the bank. Suddenly my worries come true, and I am quickly shocked back into action to find out just how bad things are.

What we are doing when we make absolutes out of these things that we worry about happening in the future is that we are really identifying the object of our trust. If we worry about our job, then we are saying that one of the major objects of trust for our future is our job. We are trusting in that job to protect our future. Or if we are worrying about money, we are placing our faith for the future in money. If we are worried about going to the top of tall buildings, we are saying that our future is based on our ability to avoid tall buildings. *That which we make an absolute is what we trust.*

Your Self-Talk gives you away. Your worries identify your security blanket for the future. But how good a job must you have? How much money must you have in the bank in order to be secure? How many floors can you go up to in a building and still feel safe? How far can you go from your home and still be safe? Do you see the difficulty? You are placing your trust in something that is of relative value! You can never have enough money. You can never know for sure if this is the best job you can have. There's always the possibility that you could have found a better job. How good must your health be to not worry about it? You never quite know if you're healthy enough. Those are all slippery objects of trust, for they never are quite solid enough.

The key to breaking the paralyzing cycle of worry and anxiety is to find something solid in which to trust. For me, the only thing worth trusting for the future is God himself. Jesus points out the obvious choice we have to make when it comes to solving the patterns of worry and anxiety. In Matthew 6:24 he says, "No one can serve two masters; for either he will hate the one and love the other, or he will be devoted to the one and despise the other. You cannot serve God and mammon." You cannot trust God for the future and at the same time worry about having enough money . . . or being healthy enough . . . or having the best possible job . . . or . . . whatever you worry about.

Jesus continues:

Therefore I tell you, do not be anxious about your life, what you shall eat or what you shall drink, nor about your body, what you shall put on. Is not life more than food, and the body more than clothing?

> Look at the birds of the air: they neither sow nor reap nor gather
> into barns, and yet your heavenly Father feeds them. Are you not of
> more value than they? And which of you by being anxious [worrying]
> can add one cubit [moment] to his span of life?
>
> Matthew 6:25–27

The obvious answer is that no one can. But we could go on with that answer and say that instead, we are really subtracting time from our lives with worry and anxiety. We are cutting life shorter rather than adding to it. To go on with Jesus's words:

> And why are you anxious about clothing? Consider the lilies of the
> field, how they grow; they neither toil nor spin; yet I tell you, even
> Solomon in all his glory was not arrayed like one of these. But if God
> so clothes the grass of the field, which today is alive and tomorrow
> is thrown into the oven, will he not much more clothe you, O men
> of little faith? Therefore do not be anxious.
>
> Matthew 6:28–31

So don't worry or be anxious about the future. For if you are all caught up in worries, you demonstrate the real object of your faith.

I used to worry about money. I tried not to elevate money to an absolute, but notice what happened. My motto was that God was always a day late and a dollar short for me. That was my Self-Talk. When I needed money, I would really try to trust God for my needs. But because I had raised money to such a level through worry, I had put God in a box. If he came through as I asked him to, then I could trust him. But when he was a day late or a dollar short, I couldn't trust him. He let me down! So I was torn between my need for money and my love for God. I have, in that experience, proven Jesus's point that I am trying to serve two masters. It can't be done.

But I finally worked through that worry by changing my Self-Talk to say that if God is the object of my trust, then if it appears to me that he is a day late and a dollar short, I won't get angry at him. I am still able to trust him to work out all the ramifications of getting that check a day late in the mail. I don't have to get caught in the trap of worry, for the battleground is still in my mind—in my Self-Talk.

The only thing worthy of trust in regard to the future is God. Paul writes in 2 Timothy 2:13 that "if we are faithless, he remains faithful—for he cannot deny himself." Even if we worry, God remains faithful to us. Even if we try to turn our back on him, he remains faithful to us. Why? Because he cannot deny his nature.

Worry is an attempt to reach into the future and to control it. We worry about having enough money, thinking that if we worry enough, we will have enough money. We worry about the kids, thinking that worrying is caring, and if we worry enough, we will be able to reach into their future and protect them. We are really trying to play God. But only God is worthy of trust. And only our trust will destroy our patterns of worry and anxiety.

One of the biggest worriers in history was Abraham. (If you are a worrier, at least you are in good company.) At the end of his life, he was known as a man of great faith. In fact, he is called the father of our faith. Let's look at how he broke the pattern of worry and learned how to trust.

Soon after we are introduced to Abraham, he goes into a new country. And he worries about what will happen to his wife, Sarah. Now she is about seventy at this time, and she must be quite a good-looking lady, for Abraham is worried and says, "When the Egyptians see you, they will say, 'This is his wife'; then they will kill me, but they will let you live" (Gen. 12:12). Abraham is all caught up in "What if . . ." Self-Talk. He is worried that the Egyptians might kill him. Of course that would have been tragic, but where is his trust? Obviously, he is trusting in himself, for he devises a plan to avoid the problem. He could have trusted in the God who earlier had promised that he would become a great nation, but instead he chooses to trust in his own ability.

He and Sarah devise a plan by which they will say that she is his sister. And in this way they will both be able to live—so they reason. But Pharaoh is so taken by this beautiful woman that he begins to court her by giving Abraham all kinds of gifts. But Pharaoh's household is afflicted with sickness, and Pharaoh sees this as a warning. He calls Abraham in and says, "What is this you have done to me? Why did you not tell me that she was your wife?" (v. 18). And they are both sent on their way.

Abraham is such a worrier that some time later he tells the king of Gerar the same story (see Gen. 20). This time the king is warned in a dream, and again Abraham creates more problems than necessary because he is a worrier. He just can't seem to trust God's integrity and power in these sticky situations where his life is threatened. In other areas his faith and trust are solid.

God finally confronts him with his worries. Abraham is asked by God to take his only son, Isaac, and offer him as a sacrifice. Apparently, he has learned to trust God more, for he is obedient to God's strange request. For some reason, God asks him to sacrifice Isaac in the land of Moriah, on a mountain there. That was a three-day journey away. Can you imagine the worry and anxiety that Abraham experiences on that trip? What kind of Self-Talk does he have during those three days?

Genesis doesn't tell us about the journey, but most likely it is a very quiet journey. And in the silence Abraham's thoughts race back over his experiences with God and with Isaac, and now he is faced with a choice. Who or what will he trust? This time he watches his mouth. He is sorting through his thoughts, trembling at the demand of God.

By the time he arrives at the appointed place, he has worked through his Self-Talk and, in the process, becomes a man of faith rather than a worrier. When they arrive, he speaks to the others with him, telling them to wait. Notice now his words in Genesis 22:5 (italics added). He says, "I and the lad will go yonder and worship, *and come again to you.*" He doesn't sound worried at this point!

A few moments later, when Isaac asks where the lamb is for the sacrifice, Abraham says, "God will provide himself the lamb for a burnt offering, my son" (v. 8). Those are words of trust, not of worry. Something has happened to change Abraham. And that change has taken place in his Self-Talk—his words and his thoughts. Abraham, the father of the faithful: a transformed worrier.

How can you do the same if you're a worrier? Here are four practical steps you can take to break the cycle of worry and anxiety.

1. *Decide to change.* Make a conscious choice to change your attitude, your behavior, and your Self-Talk. Don't decide to stop worrying. That's focusing on the wrong thing. Decide to change and keep on making that choice. You have that ability, for change is possible by gaining control of your thoughts.

2. *Work on your mouth.* My wife and I have a little signal that we give to each other when we start talking about worries. We say, "Watch your mouth." Now sometimes you can say that to your kids and it has a totally different meaning from what Jan and I mean. That's because we have agreed to use these three words as a signal to be careful about what we are saying. We say "Watch your mouth" because our words are a reflection of our thoughts—our Self-Talk. And we are talking "worry talk."

Sometimes we have to trace our worries and anxieties back to a major belief system. We may need help with this, for often the belief systems connected to our worries are operating on an implicit level. But if we track down what it is we are absolutizing (what object or principle we are fearing will be violated), we are close to the source. Then we need to see if the situation we are worried about actually involves a danger over which we have some degree of control. If not, then we attack those thoughts and remove the absolutes our worries have generated.

3. *Verbalize your faith and trust, not your doubts and worries.* If you are worried about finding a job, then you must attack the absolutes attached to your worries and replace those thoughts and verbalized words with thoughts and verbalized words of faith and trust. If you are worried about having enough money, you first attack your demands that you must have more money, and then replace those absolute demands with words and thoughts of faith and trust.

Sometimes I ask clients of mine to wear a rubber band on their wrist (one that fits rather loosely). Then, every time they begin to worry, they are to pull back the rubber band just a few inches and let it snap lightly against their wrist. (One young lady was so intent on stopping her thought patterns that she pulled the rubber band out as far as it would go and then let it snap. She came back the next week with several scabs on her wrist, and the rubber band now on her other wrist. There is no need to draw blood! Just a light sting will do it.)

Using this technique, you say in your mind the word "Stop!" If you're alone, you can say the word out loud. Then, and this is the third point, you replace that worry with some positive thought, or a promise from the Bible, that contradicts your worry.

For example, if you're worried about having enough money to pay the bills, the moment you start to worry, snap the rubber band, say "Stop!" and then repeat the verse, "And my God will supply every need of yours according to his riches in glory in Christ Jesus" (Phil.

4:19). Or if you're worried that something terrible has happened to one of your children, the moment you start to worry, snap the rubber band, say "Stop!" and then say in your mind or out loud the promise in Psalm 112:7, "He is not afraid of evil tidings; his heart is firm, trusting in the LORD." God's promises give power to your Self-Talk.

4. *Live "as if" the affirmation of faith and trust is true.* You see, you have a choice. You can live "as if," or you can live the "what ifs." The what ifs place you in the world of worry and anxiety; the as ifs place you in the world of faith and trust.

But, some might say, that's phony. No, that's faith. For faith is defined as the "assurance of things hoped for, the conviction of things not seen" (Heb. 11:1). You ask, where's the evidence? Our trust in a trustworthy God is the evidence. The only alternative is to trust in something else that is also unseen—our own ability to control the future.

That's a big order, isn't it? But you start with baby steps in one direction. Take one area of worry or anxiety and begin to replace your what-if Self-Talk with the as-if Self-Talk of trust and faith. The worries won't give up easily. You can quickly slip back into old patterns of thinking that trigger worry and fear. But those old patterns no longer control your life. You know how to let go of the future and your fears. You know how to stop worry and anxiety.

Questions for Personal Growth and Discussion

1. Who does most of the worrying in your family? Describe how they worry.

2. What are some of your worry statements?

3. What would change in your life this week if your what ifs became as ifs?

9

Gaining Control of Stress

Thou dost keep him in perfect peace,
whose mind is stayed on thee.

Isaiah 26:3

The key word for our world today is *stress*. It is a common condition that attacks us all, regardless of age. Even when we feel we are in control, stress can knock us off balance.

A study at Baylor University showed that stress alone could cause attacks in healthy hearts. A person doesn't even have to harbor feelings of anger and resentment over the years to trigger a coronary.

In the Baylor study, scientists observed two groups of pigs. One group was placed under stress for a period of time. Then both groups of animals had their coronary arteries blocked. Within minutes, the animals in the group that had experienced stress died. The animals in the other group did not die, even when the major blood supply to their hearts was blocked.

The article went on to point out that a psychological factor was necessary for the blockage to produce the death-causing heart attack. That psychological factor is stress. And it is what we are thinking or how we are thinking—or both—that creates stress.

As defined by Dr. Hans Selye, stress is "the rate of wear and tear within the body." Sometimes the stress reactions within us are so subdued that we are not even aware of them. For example, our bodies react to the stress related to the invasion of germs. The more common forms of stress are found in our environment, such as noise and air pollution, overcrowded living conditions, the pressure of deadlines and competition. In fact, stress can be defined as any event or circumstance in life that requires a person to adapt or change.

The body initially responds to stress by an alarm reaction. Changes occur throughout the body to mobilize its defenses and protect it against danger. Central to this response are the two tiny adrenal glands. A signal is released from the pituitary gland to the adrenals to release one of two types of hormones into the system. One hormone is released in the presence of sudden stress; another hormone is released with prolonged stress. They help regulate the amount and distribution of body fluids, maintain blood pressure, conserve energy, help the body cope with infection, and allow other hormones to work more effectively throughout the body. The adrenals are assisted by other glands and the body's nervous system.

That's a simplified description of the physical side of stress. The results, physically, can be either good or bad, depending on our ability to mobilize the body's defenses.

Not all stress is bad. As defined by Selye, stress involves a factor that requires us to change or adapt to change. That definition includes within itself the fact that stressors can be both positive and negative. This fact was documented in an extensive study by

Doctors T. H. Holmes and R. H. Rahe of the University of Washington Medical School. They catalogued a list of life-change events that seemed related to the onset of physical illness. Then they identified forty-three events on a Social Readjustment Rating Scale that has remarkable predictive ability for the onset of disease and disability. To use the scale, you simply indicate events that have taken place in your life during the past twelve months. Then add up the numerical values for the items checked to come up with your score.

The Social Readjustment Rating Scale

Life Event	Mean Value
1. Death of spouse	100
2. Divorce	73
3. Marital separation	65
4. Jail term	63
5. Death of close family member	63
6. Personal injury or illness	53
7. Marriage	50
8. Fired at work	47
9. Marital reconciliation	45
10. Retirement	45
11. Change in health of family member	44
12. Pregnancy	40
13. Sex difficulties	39
14. Gain of new family member	39
15. Business readjustment	39
16. Change in financial state	38
17. Death of close friend	37
18. Change to different line of work	36
19. Change in number of arguments with spouse	35
20. Mortgage over $10,000	31
21. Foreclosure of mortgage or loan	30
22. Change in responsibilities at work	29

Life Event	Mean Value
23. Son or daughter leaving home	29
24. Trouble with in-laws	29
25. Outstanding personal achievement	28
26. Wife begin or stop work	26
27. Begin or end school	26
28. Change in living conditions	25
29. Revision of personal habits	24
30. Trouble with boss	23
31. Change in work hours or conditions	20
32. Change in residence	20
33. Change in schools	20
34. Change in recreation	19
35. Change in church activities	19
36. Change in social activities	18
37. Mortgage or loan less than $10,000	17
38. Change in sleeping habits	16
39. Change in number of family get-togethers	15
40. Change in eating habits	15
41. Vacation	13
42. Christmas	12
43. Minor violations of the law	11

Reprinted by permission of the publisher from *The Journal of Psychosomatic Research,* vol. 11: T. H. Holmes and R. H. Rahe, Social Readjustment Rating Scale. Copyright © 1967 by Elsevier Science Inc.

If you score below 150 points, you are on the safe side. If you score between 150 and 300 points, your chances of becoming ill or disabled during the next two years are about 50–50. That's not too good. If you score over 300 points, you'd better make sure your health insurance is paid up, because your chances of becoming ill increase to 90 percent!

For example, let's look at a typical office supervisor. Let's call him Ken. Ken has just received a promotion (20), which has added more responsibility to his work. Along with it, Ken received a healthy raise (38), and with his wife going back to work (26), Ken decides to finally purchase their dream house (20). The new mortgage (31) will be covered by his wife's pay and his raise. His new responsibilities require a lot of entertaining, and Ken has to go on a strict diet to keep from gaining weight (15).

Unfortunately, the added stress on the job has created pressures in their marriage. Ken and his wife argue a lot more (35), and that's affected their sexual relationship adversely (39). If we stop there, Ken has accumulated 224 points, enough to put him in the 50–50 bracket. And even if he takes a vacation (13), makes an appointment with a marriage counselor to work on reconciliation (45), or asks to go back to his old job (36), it will still involve further changes and increased stress.

If we push Ken over 300 points, there is still one chance in ten that he will not get ill or disabled. Our concern is with how to be that one person in ten. And the key to surviving stress is found in our Self-Talk.

If Ken's Self-Talk sounds something like this, he's in big trouble:

I shouldn't have taken that promotion.

Why can't Mary understand the stress I'm under? (After all, she should!)

We should've waited before buying that house.

Why can't Mary simply adjust to the fact that she has to work and get off my back? (She should, you know.)

This psychologist better help her get her act together, or else our marriage won't survive! (He must, or else!)

I'd take her on a vacation, but we can't afford it. (She should understand that!)

Ken is only adding to his stress by plugging into angry feelings tied to the shoulds he is placing on Mary and on life. He's opening himself up for depression because he's putting so many demands on himself. And in the process, he is simply reinforcing the out-of-control feelings he is already fighting.

Ken could just as easily think thoughts that sound like these:

Maybe that promotion wasn't everything I thought it would be, but I worked hard for it.

Sure wish Mary understood the pressure I feel.

I'm glad we can get help for our marriage. Mary is very important to me, and I want to do everything I can to help the situation.

Somehow we'll survive what's happening, because life is good and I love my family.

Because the major factor in stress is the psychological factor, Ken's Self-Talk is the one thing he has under his control that can help him survive the stressors in his life.

The apostle Paul knew the effects of stress. He was thrown into prison numerous times, beaten and left for dead, shipwrecked, and rejected by his fellow Christians. Yet he was not only able to endure those stress points in his life, he also maintained an attitude that has inspired the church through the centuries that followed.

In 2 Corinthians 4 Paul writes, "We are afflicted in every way, but not crushed; perplexed, but not driven to despair; persecuted, but not forsaken; struck down, but not destroyed" (vv. 8–9). Paul could have stopped there, put his pen down, and reflected on how hard his life had been. If his Self-Talk was one of self-pity, he would have given added power to the stress he was describing. But that's not Paul's response.

He continues, "So we do not lose heart. Though our outer nature is wasting away, our inner nature is being renewed every day" (v. 16). Paul almost gives us Selye's definition of stress when he talks about his outer nature, his body, wasting away. Paul endured great wear and tear on his body. Yet he did not give in to stress, for he adds that his inner nature, his mind and spirit, was being renewed every day. We've already seen how Paul renewed his mind by capturing every thought and bringing it into obedience to Christ. Paul knew how to take the stressors of his life and turn them around to his advantage. His secret was in his Self-Talk.

We can see this in action as we follow Paul in the Book of Acts. In chapter 16 he and his partner, Silas, are placed in a Macedonian prison. While there, Paul captures his thoughts by focusing on those things worthy of praise. He and Silas spend their time praying and singing hymns to God. He renews his inner nature, in the face of stress, through his Self-Talk.

Several times he is beaten. He is shipwrecked and then placed under arrest in Rome. While in prison there, he writes several of the letters in the New Testament. One is to the Philippians; and in that letter he several times urges them to *rejoice* in everything. Then he adds the comment that he has learned to be content in whatever state he is in (Phil. 4:11)! How does he do that in the face of so much stress? Only one way—by the renewal of his mind.

In that same letter to the Philippians, Paul describes the kind of attitude he wants his readers to experience. He writes, "Your attitude should be the kind that was shown us by Jesus Christ, who, though he was God, did not *demand* and cling to his rights as God, but laid aside his mighty power and glory, taking the disguise of a slave and becoming like men" (Phil. 2:5–7 TLB, italics added).

Here is Paul's secret weapon against stress. In his Self-Talk he aims at developing the same attitude that he sees in Jesus. In that attitude, the demands for his rights are set aside. He lives in the attitude of a servant. Paul's Self-Talk is centered on the example and character of Jesus Christ. And as Isaiah notes, the person whose mind is stayed (or focused) on God will experience perfect peace.

Perfect peace in the midst of stress! How can we learn to be survivors in a stress-filled civilization? How can we develop the same attitude shown to us by Jesus Christ? Here are several steps you can take to begin to change your Self-Talk and gain control of stress.

1. *Identify stressful situations in your life.* You've already started that process in the past three chapters. Situations that trigger feelings of anger, depression, worry, or anxiety are all stress-creating situations. Or you might identify stressors by looking at what you avoid in your job or at home. What people, situations, jobs, or tasks do you wish would disappear from your life?

For example, Jane is feeling extremely nervous and tense today. She is angry with one of her coworkers, arguing with her boss over her latest assignment, overwhelmed by the unfinished projects at home, and tomorrow afternoon has to make a special presentation to a high-level committee at work. Jane might include on her list things like:

Stressful Situations

1. Angry with Larry over his put-down at lunch.
2. Frustrated with Tom over the new job he's given me.
3. Should replant the flower garden.
4. South side of the house must be painted.
5. Scared to death over this committee meeting tomorrow.
6. Must get the kids to clean up the garage.

Now make your list, and be as specific as possible. Don't take the time now to wonder why those specific things bother you or even how you are going to fix them; just make a detailed list.

When your list seems complete, look it over and try to see if there are any similarities between items on the list. For example, you may notice a number of situations in which you are called on to make decisions. Or you may have several items that relate to your being evaluated by others or that tie into feelings of competitiveness. Write down these common themes.

2. *Take one of those events, or one theme, and begin to work on your Self-Talk.* To do this, begin by identifying how this stressful person or situation is threatening or frightening you. What are you saying to yourself already in your Self-Talk that triggers those feelings of threat and stress?

For example, Jane might look over her list and see that the most urgent stressor she is feeling is the meeting tomorrow. So she begins to identify her negative Self-Talk. She lists these statements on the left side of a piece of paper, and they might look something like this:

Negative Self-Talk

1. I hate these kinds of meetings.

2. I'll make a fool of myself.

3. I can't talk in front of groups.

4. I'll get all tense and blow it.

5. I'll probably even knock over the flip-chart.

6. Why did Tom ask me to do this?

Now write down your thoughts and statements on the left side of a sheet of paper. Again, be as specific as you possibly can. Look for the demands in your Self-Talk, as well as the absolutes like "never" and "always."

Then put the sheet away for a while and go on to step number 3.

3. *Use your imagination to visualize yourself in that situation without an experience of stress or threat.* Our mental pictures are a part of our Self-Talk and have great potential for changing us. Our stress and negative Self-Talk are often crystallized by mental images we create in our imagination. Changing those mental images releases power for change. Therefore, seeing ourselves coping or changing can help us make that behavior a reality.

To do this, you begin by selecting one of the stressful situations you want to change. Probably the one you analyzed in step 2 would be a good choice. Then set aside between fifteen and thirty minutes when no one will disturb you.

The next step is to find a place to lie down, close your eyes, and be comfortable. Take some time to relax, using deep breathing or by progressively relaxing the muscles in your body by first tensing a group of muscles, then letting them relax. Some people do this by starting with their toes, relaxing those muscles, and then moving up their body slowly, making sure every muscle is as relaxed as possible. As you become very relaxed, be sure your mind stays alert while directing the relaxation process. Enjoy the feelings of relaxation!

Another way to help your body relax is to picture in your mind a beautiful, tranquil scene. One of the scenes some people use is a beautiful beach on a tropical island. Others love the mountains and enjoy picturing a beautiful valley in the spring, with the lush green meadow broken only by the colors of the wild flowers. Perhaps there is a brook gurgling nearby, and the trees bend gently in the whispering wind as songbirds flutter from tree to tree.

When you have this scene painted in your imagination, move yourself into the picture you're imagining. Sit by a tree, or if you're on a beach, sit alone on a long stretch of white sand near some bending palm trees. Watch the gentle waves come to the shore as you sit there. Try to hear the wind and feel the sun's warmth. Then concentrate on the details of the scene, noticing the flowers or the patterns in the sand. Be there—as if you are really there.

Finally, when you are relaxed, keeping your eyes closed, move from that relaxing place in the mountains or by the ocean to the stressful situation you have selected. But instead of seeing yourself pressured and hassled by the stress to the point of total distress, try to imagine ways of changing that situation. See yourself reacting differently to the people in that situation. As you see things differently, change the patterns of your thoughts and think of yourself as coping successfully with the stress. Visualize yourself experiencing feelings of self-control and self-confidence. Try to see as many details as possible, including the behavior and attitudes of the other people involved.

When Jane tries this, she tells her family that she wants to be left alone for about thirty minutes. She retreats into the bedroom and stretches out on the bed. She has a light on as she begins to concentrate on visualizing a beautiful place in the mountains. After about ten minutes, Jane begins to picture herself at the next day's meeting. She sees herself at her desk, nervous and light-headed, just before she is scheduled to go into the meeting. She feels a lump in her throat.

But she immediately takes in a deep breath and lets it out slowly. She visualizes herself doing this at her desk, as she literally takes a slow, deep breath now. As she gets up to walk to the conference room, she tells herself to just relax and speak naturally without trying to judge her performance. She may even remind herself that these people are just normal human beings like herself.

Then, with another slow, deep breath, Jane visualizes herself entering the conference room. As she starts to make her report, she is relaxed and confident. She listens in her mind to her report and is impressed with the points she makes. She is calm, in control. She feels relaxed.

Jane may imagine the scene several times, each time watching herself act confidently and calmly. Then she gradually opens her eyes, and in a moment she rejoins her family. Already she feels the calming effect of the relaxation process.

If your stressful situation involves members of your family, perhaps one of your children, try to see the situation from their point of view. What do they see happening in the situation? Try to visualize what they are feeling. See them as scared and vulnerable. As you do this, you may notice your own perceptions of the situation changing. That's a crucial step in the process of controlling stress.

Do this for five or ten minutes, then slowly open your eyes. You probably won't want to move for a minute or two. Stay still. That's a good sign—just continue to enjoy the relaxed feelings for a while.

Sometimes a situation cannot be altered. You still are not helpless in that situation. Instead of visualizing yourself making positive changes in the situation, you may be limited to seeing yourself successfully coping with the stress. If this is the case, then visualize the stressful situation for as long as possible. Then, keeping your eyes closed, take yourself back to that tranquil place, either the beach or the mountains. Stay there in your imagination until you feel relaxed again, and then go back to the stressful scene. Again, stay as long as you can before returning to the tranquil scene, and then take some time to relax and feel calm and confident before opening your eyes.

Seeing yourself successfully coping with the stress might involve trying to understand the feelings and attitudes of the other people involved. Or you might try to identify Self-Talk statements you can make to yourself that would help you cope with the stress.

Now you're ready for the final step.

4. *Go back to your sheet of paper, and on the right-hand side rewrite the negative Self-Talk statements into positive Self-Talk statements.* You are now able to do this because in your imagination you have seen yourself successfully cope with the stress situation.

Jane is able to go back to her list of negative Self-Talk items and rewrite the statements something like this:

Negative Self-Talk	Positive Self-Talk
I hate these kinds of meetings.	I usually don't like these meetings, but this time I'm looking forward to it.
I'll make a fool of myself.	I'm not afraid of doing anything foolish. The other people there are not judging me.
I can't talk in front of groups.	I usually don't like to talk to groups, but I'm prepared and what I have to say is important.
I'll get all tense and blow it.	I know how to relieve my tension. There is no reason for me to blow it.

Now work on your list of positive Self-Talk statements. You might also spend time, daily, working on a diary of stress situations to identify the stress-producing Self-Talk. Then spend time using your imagination, through guided imagery, and watch yourself successfully cope with or change these situations. Gradually, you will be able to reduce the negative effects of stress in your life and use stress as a positive force, enabling you to achieve your dreams in life.

It is said that the Chinese word for *crisis* is written by combining the symbols for the words *danger* and *opportunity.* Stress is the same: both a danger and an opportunity, a friend and a foe. By watching your Self-Talk, you can determine which it will be for you.

Questions for Personal Growth and Discussion

1. Describe your guided imagery experience to someone. Tell what changes you experienced.

2. Identify a key word or phrase related to your guided imagery that you could repeat to yourself in a stressful situation. How would that word or phrase help you?

3. How would you relate the relaxation technique to your anger or worry?

TEN

Assertive Living through Self-Talk

Speaking the truth in love, . . .

Ephesians 4:15

One of the most interesting applications being made of popular psychology is in the assertiveness training seminars being offered throughout the country. Most adult-education programs offer a class on assertiveness, and people who have been through the training are enthusiastic. Even though many of the graduates do not always use the assertive skills they learn, they are still excited about the training because they have a better understanding of their rights and their emotions.

Unfortunately, assertiveness training is often judged by its problems. Because much assertiveness training overlooks the role of Self-Talk, people taking the courses often find themselves trapped in one of the pitfalls. When this occurs, it is usually the family of those who have taken the course that end up wishing the training had never been offered. These family members equate assertiveness with becoming angry. "All they did was show my wife how to express her anger!" a frustrated husband recently said to me. He was referring to the changes that took place in his normally calm and contented wife. From his perspective, she was changing into a tornado, telling everyone exactly what she thinks. That husband's experience is so common that people usually equate assertive behavior with aggressive behavior.

What happens in these situations is that people who have usually been rather passive about life suddenly find out that they have some rights in any given situation. But their pattern of passiveness has led them to store up their anger, which now comes boiling over the top of their emotions. These quiet people are suddenly aggressive. And their aggressive behavior, along with the awareness of their anger, scares them. They don't want to be angry or aggressive. Very quickly, they get their assertive skills confused with aggressiveness, and in frustration they retreat back into their passive behavior patterns.

In order to put assertiveness into the proper perspective, let's look at the differences among these three approaches to life: passiveness, aggressiveness, and assertiveness.

Passiveness

Passive approaches to life are usually attached to the emotion of fear. As we have seen, emotions are created by our Self-Talk. So the passive person is usually saying in his or her Self-Talk things like:

I can't say no. I'd feel so guilty.

I can't tell my husband to spend more time with me. He'd only get angry.

I can't take this blouse back to the store. They'd only tell me to make sure I get the right size next time.

I don't want to make a fuss, so I'll just go along with my company's new policy.

I can't complain to the manager about the service; no one else seems to mind.

No need to defend myself and make a fool of myself. I'll probably never see this other person again.

These are just a few examples of what becomes a way of life for many people. In their passive approach to people and events, they end up violating their own rights by failing to face their honest feelings and thoughts. By being apologetic and self-effacing, they have allowed other people to violate them. What their Self-Talk is really saying is, "I don't count! So go ahead and take advantage of me!" In the process, passive people soon lose any sense of self-respect—or they create a boiling cauldron of anger and resentment within that's just waiting to explode.

Aggressiveness

As long as people can remain passive, their goal is to appease others and avoid any conflict, regardless of the cost. Sometimes, though, the pent-up anger and resentment do explode, and then we have an aggressive person. This person's Self-Talk sounds something like this:

No way will I do that! And besides, I'm tired of everyone expecting me to say yes!

What's the matter with you? Don't you know I have rights too! You'd better spend more time with me or else!

Some stupid salesclerk gave me the wrong size. I demand my
money back now!

Just who do you think you are, talking to me like that?

I'm so fed up with the way things are done around here. Go
ahead and fire me; see if I care!

At least aggressive people stand up for their rights, but look
at how they do it! They express thoughts and feelings in a way
that now violates the other person's rights and feelings. Aggressive people's desire is to dominate in such a way that they can
ensure themselves of winning. Their angry Self-Talk leads them
to use humiliation, belittling, or overpowering tactics—anything
to gain victory. Their Self-Talk is now dominated by the thought
"You don't count!"

Passive people are usually trying to either *suppress* their feelings or simply *repress* and deny what they feel. When we attempt
to handle our feelings this way, the result is like stuffing more and
more items into a bag. Soon something gives, and our emotions
spill out all over the place.

Sometimes passive people, in their Self-Talk, justify their tem-
porary angry outburst by thoughts and statements that say they've
earned the right to be angry. It's as if they have taken so much abuse,
and have had their own rights violated so many times, that they now
have a trading-stamp book filled and ready to be redeemed. And
the prize they want to claim is the right to be angry. What usually
happens is that there is a tax on that prize called guilt.

Aggressive people are no longer denying or suppressing their
emotions; they're now *expressing* them loud and clear. If you're
on the receiving end of that expression, you have the feeling that
the whole time they are venting their anger, they have their finger
pointed at you. The expression of emotion often has with it the

element of accusation. That's why we react so defensively when someone is being aggressive with us.

Usually, people react aggressively when they themselves feel threatened. Their Self-Talk urges them to "get" the other person before the other person has an advantage. At other times, people can act aggressively because the current situation reminds them of a past emotional experience that is still unresolved.

In both the passive and the aggressive reactions to people or situations, those caught in these behavior patterns do not feel good about themselves afterwards. This is because the passive and the aggressive behavior are reactions to events or other people. Whenever we react to something, we experience that old out-of-control feeling. The situation is determining our behavior—we are only able to react.

Assertiveness

Assertiveness is different. It is neither passive nor aggressive. It is neither motivated by fear nor by anger. True assertive behavior is motivated by the emotion of love. You care enough about yourself and about others that you will speak up for your rights and be careful not to violate anyone else's rights at the same time. In my work with Dr. Frank Freed, we describe this handling of emotions as *confession*. We do not repress, suppress, or express our emotions. We confess them.

In the Greek, the meaning of the word *confess* is "to agree with." When you confess your feelings and emotions, you are verbally agreeing with what you feel inside. When you confess these emotions and feelings, you are describing to another person what is going on inside of you.

One of the mistakes often encountered in attitudes regarding assertiveness is that it is a way to get what you want. You cannot do that with assertiveness! Perhaps by being aggressive that goal could be accomplished. But with assertiveness, the major reason for acting assertively is that you regain that sense of self-control. You are not pushing someone else around at his or her expense, and you are not being pushed around—both ways of reacting to life. You are now experiencing self-control and are able to *act* the way you choose, not *react!* This eventually leads you to greater feelings of self-confidence and self-control, which reduce your need to be either passive or aggressive. And since assertiveness is motivated by the emotion of love, your goal in acting assertively is to maximize the possibility that all parties in a situation are able to partially achieve their goals. This leads to a closer, more satisfying type of relationship with others. Once again, the battle for asser-tive behavior begins in your mind—in your Self-Talk. Nonassert-ive people are dominated in their Self-Talk by shoulds, and these shoulds lead to feelings of "I can't."

Whenever you nonassertively say or think "I should," you set in motion the following:

I Immobilization

S Saying—not doing

H Hung up on guilt

O Overly anxious

U Underlying anger

L Lowered self-esteem

D Depression

That's not a satisfying pattern at all. Nonassertive behavior pat-terns feed right into feelings of guilt, anger, worry, anxiety, and depression. The result is always a lowering of self-esteem and a feeling of being paralyzed. You sit and talk about what you should have done. Or you sit and brood about what you shouldn't have done. And nothing happens to change you or the situation—you're paralyzed.

The I shoulds always lead to the I can'ts. The I can'ts create the following pattern:

I Inadequate feelings about myself

C Controlled instead of being in control

A Apathetic

N Negative results

T Total despair

No wonder you say "I can't!" You're inadequate, out of control, and tired of negative results to what you do attempt, which leads you to become even more apathetic, until you give up in total despair.

Four *D*s of Assertive Living

So what can you do? Let me describe for you the four *D*s of assertive living. This is a way to monitor your Self-Talk, turning it into a force for change.

Describe:
First, sit down and describe the kinds of situations in which you react nonassertively. Take the time to write out the description of the conflict.

Define:
Second, define what is happening to you. What are you saying, doing, and thinking? What is your Self-Talk? What are your expectations

in this situation? Define as clearly as possible your feelings, fears, hostilities, and behavior.

Discern:

Third, try to discern what the other person, or persons, may be thinking. What might be their motives? What might they be feeling? What is going on inside the others involved in this situation?

Decide:

Fourth, make a decision about what you *can* do about this situation. What new assertive strategy can you use to break out of the trap you feel caught in? What one thing can you begin doing differently in love, which would create the possibility of change?

Try it right now. Don't listen to those old patterns of Self-Talk that say it *can't* be done. Become a believer in "I can!" The "I can" pattern looks like this:

I Initiate change by acting, not reacting

C Confess my feelings

A Ask for what I want and need

N Negotiate for positive results

You can begin to initiate that change by filling in the following Four-*D*s chart for one specific pattern of behavior.

Describe:

Define:

Discern:

Decide:

Continued assertive behavior is based on Self-Talk that believes you have a right to self-respect and respect from other people. Since your motivating emotion is love, you are concerned about the other person's self-respect and rights. You are able to show this respect by "speaking the truth in love." In other words, you are honest to yourself and to others about what you feel, and you confess these feelings in direct and appropriately caring ways.

Assertive Self-Talk sounds something like this:

> I have committed myself to all I can handle right now. I have the right to say no.
>
> I have a right to let my husband know he is hurting me by his silence. I love him too much to keep that a secret.
>
> I paid for this blouse, and I have the right to get my money's worth. If it doesn't fit, I have the right to take it back and at least get a credit.
>
> The service here really is bad. The manager needs to know that people are dissatisfied.

The best model of assertive living was Jesus. He was always in control. When he experienced anger, he dealt with it. When Jesus went to the tomb of his friend Lazarus, he was deeply moved, and those feelings of grief were seen in his behavior and his words. When, just before his own death, he encountered emotions of fear, he retreated to the garden and described in prayer the heaviness he felt within. Then he went out and faced the cross.

Jesus always spoke directly and honestly about what he was feeling. He spoke out for justice; demonstrated by word and behavior his firm belief in the value of each individual; loved deeply and passionately; refused to honor dishonesty; refused to be intimidated; and then told us to love ourselves and others the same way.

Paul acted assertively when he stood up to Peter, confronting him about his wishy-washiness in eating with the Gentiles only as long as the Jewish Christians were not present (see Gal. 2:11–21). He could have stood off to the side, thinking that if he confronted Peter, Peter might get angry with him—or that some other people might get upset with him. That would have been a passive response to the situation.

Paul could also have reacted aggressively, becoming hostile with Peter and entering into a shouting match that would have embarrassed both of them. But Paul was motivated by love, so he assertively confronted Peter. That he could speak openly about that event in his letter to the Galatians indicates he felt all right about his behavior afterwards—a good sign that a person has acted assertively.

In every case of assertive behavior, the person has developed Self-Talk based on a belief system that includes the following five points:

1. Every person has the right to be respected by others and also has the right to self-respect.
2. Every person has needs, but no one has the right to demand that you sacrifice your needs for their needs.
3. Every person has feelings. And everyone has the right to confess these feelings in a way that does not violate the rights of another person.
4. Every person has opinions. And everyone has the right to properly express those opinions.
5. Every person has the right to make decisions and has the right to live with those decisions.

You can see that each point affirms the self-worth of an individual. Assertive living is always based on the emotion of love, not on anger or fear. When you are living assertively, you are motivated and inspired to action because you feel good about yourself and about life. You are living in the I cans of life.

Questions for Personal Growth and Discussion

1. Try to identify times when you have been passive, aggressive, and assertive. Which approach best describes your general pattern?

2. When you have reacted aggressively, describe how other people involved might have felt. When you have reacted passively, describe how you felt.

3. How would love change your experience of passive or aggressive behavior into assertive behavior? Give examples.

ELEVEN

Self-Talk

Faith or Presumption?

The nations rage, the kingdoms totter;
he utters his voice, the earth melts.

Psalm 46:6

The power released by our Self-Talk is incredible. Not only do our thoughts and words create our emotions, they have the power to make us well or sick and to determine our future.

This renewed emphasis on the power of the mind reflects a swing back to ancient ideas concerning the interrelationship of the body and the mind. The seventeenth-century French philosopher René Descartes challenged the dominant teaching of his day that the mind was dominant over the body by placing great importance on the body. Descartes emphasized that the body was like a machine, "so built up and composed of nerves, muscles, veins, blood and

179

skin, that though there were no mind in it at all, it would not cease to have the same [functions]."

To Descartes, the mind was limited to thought and consciousness, which included the will, feelings, understandings, and what he called the passions—love, desire, hatred, hope. The mind was subject to reason and to God, but the body was only subject to mechanical laws. Even though the mind and the body interacted, it was purely a machinelike process. In reality, the two were separate.

In the years since, Descartes's ideas have dominated the fields of medicine and psychology. As a result, we have struggled with problems in the mind and in the body, wondering whether to treat the mind or the body first, but always approaching the problem with an either/or attitude. When medical science can't find a biological cause for an illness, it is put in the psychosomatic illness category. This often causes a problem for the patient, for that diagnosis is usually understood as an imaginary illness.

Today, however, we are not only seeing that the body and the mind are connected, we are seeing them as intricately intertwined. The mind can create terminal illness as well as health. It can create feelings of rage and intense hostility that not only activate the body but can also harm the body. Recently, a study headed up by University of Iowa Medical School neurobiology researchers has identified what are called "traceable physical pathways" that are responsible for our emotional reactions. Feelings involve a perception of both body changes and cognitive changes triggered by our subjective evaluation of an event in terms of similar earlier events. A tiny part of the brain called the amygdala plays an important role in our ability to experience our own emotions as well as our ability to identify the emotions someone else is experiencing. This research, according to the report, overturns the false dichotomy between mind and body created by Descartes.[4]

Another study that ties together both the body and the mind focused on blindness in female survivors of Cambodia's holocaust. During the late 1970s under the rule of Pol Pot and the Khmer Rouge, in a nation of only eight million people, almost the entire population was tortured, and over one million people were murdered. Some escaped to Thailand and eventually made their way to the United States. Of those who came to this country, a study was done on the nearly hundred and fifty Cambodian women of middle age who had presented themselves to medical clinics between 1982 and 1989 because of blindness. All had been victims of the Khmer Rouge, but none knew any of the others. Since all diseases that can cause blindness are detectable, the doctors were amazed, both at the number of victims as well as at the total lack of any physiological basis for the blindness in so many women. The report stated that "in the annals of war, no other descriptions occur of a number of people isolated from each other losing their sight for reasons that no one can explain."[5] If there was no physical basis to the blindness, then only the mind could be responsible. More and more the mind is being identified as the center of self-control.

The God-Is-My-Genie Syndrome

With this renewed emphasis on the power of the mind and the role our thoughts and words play, it becomes easy to slide into some problems. We can be fooled into believing that if we can master our thoughts, we can be the captain of our fate! And if we press this point far enough, we can soon believe that if we want a new Cadillac, we can speak it into being. Or if we want to be rich, we think right and grow rich. If we are sick, we visualize ourselves becoming well—and we become well. Suddenly, we feel like Aladdin must have felt when he discovered that the lamp he found contained a magic genie. Nothing is impossible!

Sounds great—sounds even better when you hear it from a "faith teacher" or a positive-motivational preacher. And the message will work. At least some of the time.

I talked with a couple in my office recently who had been through what they called the "faith talk" process. They had been listening to a group of preachers and teachers who had tied together many of the same verses from the Bible I've referred to. But in the process they had created a system that can easily be used to attempt to turn God into a genie-like being.

As we talked about their experience, they related how they had been taught that words had power and that whatever they said would come true. For a time they were excited about the principles of faith talk, for it had given substance to their faith.

But as they sat talking with me, I could see they were now bitter and confused. They told me about their daughter, who had recently dropped out of college. For several years they had been concerned about Lori's behavior and attitudes. She had a pattern of choosing friends whose values were in complete contradiction to her values and those of her parents. But Lori managed to finish high school with decent grades and even made plans to attend college.

About the time Lori went off to college, her parents started practicing affirming their faith in God's ability to get Lori's life straightened around. They practiced it in the way they prayed, always thanking God for what he "had already done." They practiced faith talk whenever they spoke about Lori, again affirming carefully only the kinds of behavior and attitudes they were trusting God to create within her.

They were especially concerned about Lori's attitude toward sexual behavior, so this became the focus of their confessions of faith, both in conversations together and in their prayers. They guarded their words carefully so as not to give power to any negative forms of behavior in Lori's life.

For six months they had felt an emotional release through changing their thoughts and their words in reference to Lori. Faith talk had worked! At least it had worked until a couple of days earlier when Lori arrived home unexpectedly.

After several days of silent brooding, Lori finally admitted she had been kicked out of college because she had been arrested with a group of her friends for possession of drugs. And then, as if that confession broke the dam on her emotions, she poured out the details of how her boyfriend had broken up with her after she told him she was pregnant.

As Lori's parents related the story to me, the bitterness and anger they felt against the faith teachers and against God began to spill over as well.

"What did we do wrong?" they demanded. "Didn't we believe enough? We can't remember doubting or speaking about any negative things for Lori. Why did God let us down?" Then they waited in silence, wanting answers for their crumbling faith. After all, hadn't God promised that "he shall have whatever he saith" (see Mark 11:23 KJV)?

Lori's parents had taken the principles and carried them out to the letter. Unfortunately, they were left with nothing but broken hearts. At least their pain wasn't as final and tragic as that experienced by the parents of Wesley Parker. In their book, *We Let Our Son Die,* the Parkers tell about a similar struggle with words, faith, and God.

In a service in their church, their son Wesley, a diabetic, told his parents that God had healed him of his diabetes. As he had been taught, he began to speak the words of healing, affirming both in his thoughts and in his words that his diabetes was healed.

Some time later, with the encouragement of friends and of Wesley, the parents threw away his insulin. In the days that followed, Wesley showed signs of untreated diabetes. As he became sicker, groups of people from the church gathered to pray and join with Wesley in claiming the promise that he was healed. The only weakness in their faith seemed to be the questions they had about how much more faith was needed to ensure that God would keep his promise.

Even after Wesley died, the family and a group of friends firmly believed that God would bring the boy back to life. Their "resurrection" service attracted the attention of the news media across the country. And when the authorities arrested the parents, that made news as well.

Perhaps the Parkers asked questions similar to those asked by Lori's parents. Perhaps as the Parkers sat in jail, their questions were mixed with tears of bitterness over their failure to understand.

During the trial something was said that triggered an awareness in the Parkers that what they had done was not done in faith but rather was an example of presumptuousness. In the course of testimony, one witness suggested that presumption rushes out ahead of God, demanding results. Faith simply rests, leaving the results in God's hands. In hindsight, it was easy for the Parkers to see they had acted presumptuously by demanding and insisting that their son be healed.

God Is beyond Any Formula

How does one make the distinction between the power released through Self-Talk and presumption? Let's look at Paul again, since he was so helpful in setting the principles for Self-Talk. In reading through his letters, we see clearly that Paul is a realist. When things are bad, he makes verbal comments on their being bad. For example, in 1 Corinthians 4:10–13 Paul writes that "we are fools for Christ's sake. . . . We are weak. . . . We [are] in disrepute. To the present hour we hunger and thirst, we are ill-clad and buffeted and homeless, and we labor. . . . We have become, and are now, as the refuse of the world, the offscouring of all things."

Someone better say to Paul, "Watch your mouth!" After all, he is giving power to those negative feelings and circumstances. Isn't that an example of negative Self-Talk and of a poor belief system? Is Paul being masochistic in saying these things and speaking them into existence?

Paul answers these questions for us later on when he writes, "Now I rejoice in my sufferings for your sake" (Col. 1:24). Here's balance. Paul is a realist. He can acknowledge suffering when there is suffering. He can admit defeat when he's defeated. He can rest in God's ability to take care of him.

But that doesn't satisfy some who boldly assert that if Paul had fully understood the importance of thoughts and the power released by his words, he could have changed his Self-Talk and wouldn't have had to suffer. But what do these teachers do with Jesus's statements about suffering (John 16:33), about persecution (Matt. 5:11), and about the cruel form of death predicted for at least one of his followers (John 21:18–19)? Would they be so bold as to assert that Jesus didn't fully understand the importance of his words?

This is not to deny anything we've said thus far about Self-Talk. We are just making a serious effort to put Self-Talk into perspective in order to avoid putting God into a box or into a genie's bottle. When we use Self-Talk, or what Lori's parents called faith talk, to make God a prisoner of a formula, he is no longer the creative Lord of the universe. Instead, he's tucked away in a box, waiting to act on our command.

YOU ARE WHAT YOU THINK

We're still left with the questions Lori's parents asked. What makes the difference? How can we keep from being presumptuous?

Faith *in* God versus Faith *of* God

To answer that, we must look at the types of faith available to us. In Matthew 13 Jesus tells us the parable about the sower. In that parable he identifies four types of faith. One type is really no faith at all, for the seed never takes root. The second type of faith is that which quickly takes root but doesn't endure. The third type of faith takes root but is choked out by the cares of the world. Only the fourth type of faith takes root and flourishes.

It seems clear that both Lori's and Wesley's parents had that fourth type of faith. They believed and practiced their faith. But their faith became presumption because of another element. Dr. Charles Farah, in his book *From the Pinnacle of the Temple*, makes a distinction between faith *in* God and the faith *of* God. Faith in God is an objective type of faith. It is expressed in the objective case, directed toward God, and based on his ability, not on some formula. When God is the object of our faith, we are exercising faith in God. As believers we have this objective faith in God. But our human limitations keep us from ever possessing this faith in any absolute, complete way. This leaves us in a struggle, sometimes vacillating between this faith in God and our own tendency to question and doubt. In this struggle we can lose sight of who the object of our faith really is, and in those times we are overwhelmed by our doubts.

We can strengthen this objective faith through focusing our Self-Talk. This becomes our antidote to doubt: capturing our thoughts and centering them on the nature and character of a faithful God.

The danger comes when we assume that we possess the faith *of* God. This is a subjective type of faith, expressed in the subjective case. It is a special kind of faith, given by God in a specific situation and for a specific purpose. It is not a general type of faith. When we take events and examples of great faith and attempt to generalize them to apply to everyone or anyone, we are acting presumptuously. This is what Lori's parents did. They took a principle and changed it into a general demand. They did not rest in their requests, but demanded that God do what they said. That's presumption. The same is true of Wesley's parents. They took a specific principle of faith and applied it in a general way, demanding by their behavior and attitude that God do what they said.

That would be like the Israelites, following the battle of Jericho, saying that now they had the formula. Whenever they came to a walled city, they would simply march around it the proper number of times, blow trumpets, and the walls would have to fall down. Obviously, they didn't follow that pattern, for that would have been presumptuous. God had given them specific instructions for one city, Jericho. Those instructions did not apply anywhere else.

Or one might imagine Naaman the leper. Following his healing by dipping in the Jordan River seven times, he could set up a concession for healing lepers. First he could hold classes, demonstrating the prior belief systems on dipping. Then he would demonstrate how to properly dip in the Jordan River. Finally, each leper would get to dip in the Jordan River seven times in order to be healed. But that wasn't a formula! God gave Naaman a specific direction for him alone. It was a subjective faith, given to him by God for that occasion.

George Mueller had this kind of subjective, God-given faith. Every day the orphans under his care had food to eat. Yet not once did George Mueller make known his needs to anyone, with the exception of God. His unique gift of faith was special for that situation. True, it has inspired faith in countless people in the years that have followed, just as the story of Naaman has inspired faith in others. But it would be presumptuous to assert that that type of faith is available in a general way to anyone willing to learn how to "speak something into existence." We cannot find any instance in Mueller's biography in which he demanded something from God; he simply rested on God's ability to provide.

The solution to the problem of faith versus presumption boils down to the difference between demanding and resting. That difference is determined by our understanding of God, his power, and his sovereignty. To help us understand this better, let's look again at Job.

Earlier, I pointed out that the opportunity for Job's pain and suffering is created by his worries. When he says, "What I always feared has come upon me," he reveals himself as a worrier. And his worry is caused by an inadequate view of God.

All through the book of Job, his friends try to get him to see that the common theology of that day clearly points out the fact that his suffering is due to his sin. Only when people do wrong do they suffer. So, as his friends insist, he must have sinned somewhere. And if he will simply admit that fact, he will get better. They miss the point!

But to say that the reason Job suffered is because he "worried it into existence" will also miss the point. It is true, but it is only partial truth. Job's suffering has a purpose, and it transcends his problem of worry. It is directly related to his inadequate view of God.

Notice what happens when God breaks his silence. After years of self-justification, Job finally hears the Lord's answer. But what an answer! God responds to Job with a series of questions and a rebuke:

> Who is this that darkens counsel
>   by words without knowledge?
> Gird up your loins like a man,
>   I will question you, and you shall declare to me.
>
> Job 38:2–3

It doesn't sound as though God has much sympathy for Job's pain. Yet God has a purpose in all this suffering. And he directs Job to that purpose by a series of questions—profound questions that can't be answered, such as:

> Where were you when I laid the
>   foundation of the earth?
> Tell me, if you have understanding.
> Who determined its measurements—surely you know!
> Or who stretched the line upon it?
> On what were its bases sunk,
>   or who laid its cornerstone,
> when the morning stars sang together,
>   and all the sons of God shouted for joy?
>
> verses 4–7

In chapter 40 God then asks,

> Shall a faultfinder contend with the Almighty?
> He who argues with God, let him answer it.
>
> verse 2

And Job wisely says,

> Behold, I am of small account;
>   what shall I answer thee?
> I lay my hand on my mouth.
>
> verse 4

You can almost see Job putting his hand over his mouth, as if to say, "I'll shut up from now on!" But God continues with the questions. He asks,

> Will you even put me in the wrong?
>> Will you condemn me that you may be justified?
> Have you an arm like God,
>> and can you thunder with a voice like his?
>
> verses 8–9

Then God's questions continue to confront Job with the power and dominion of God over all creation. Finally, we read in chapter 42 that, when God stops the questions, Job once again answers the Lord:

> I know that thou canst do all things,
>> and that no purpose of thine can be thwarted.
> "Who is this that hides counsel without knowledge?"
>> [you ask]
> Therefore [I answer] I have uttered what I did not
>> understand,
> things too wonderful for me,
>> which I did not know. . . .
> I had heard of thee by the hearing of the ear,
>> but now my eye sees thee;
> therefore I despise myself,
>> and repent in dust and ashes.
>
> verses 2–3, 5–6

Job repent? But for what? For worrying? Hardly! I believe he is repenting for his limited understanding of God. For in his statement he admits to the fact that prior to his suffering he had known about God "by the hearing of the ear." But now he says he *knows* God because he has seen God's power, majesty, and dominion. He now has an intimate understanding of God. Job would now be able to say, as Paul later wrote, "He said to me, 'My grace is sufficient for you, for my power is made perfect in weakness'" (see 2 Cor. 12:9). He could also say with Paul, "I have learned, in whatever state I am, to be content" (Phil. 4:11).

The disciples operated on the same belief system that Job's comforters pressed on Job. Looking at a man who has been blind from birth, they ask, "Rabbi, who sinned, this man or his parents, that he was born blind?" (John 9:2). They might have asked, "Whose negative thoughts and words caused this suffering?" Either way, Jesus's answer clearly puts Self-Talk, faith, and presumption into perspective: "It was not that this man sinned, or his parents, but *that the works of God might be made manifest in him*" (John 9:3, italics added).

But what can we say to Lori's parents? First, we need to help them see the distinction between demanding and resting. *Presumption demands; faith rests.* As we have clearly seen in every chapter, we create problems in our Self-Talk when we begin to make demands. Lori's parents were using the principles of faith talk to place shoulds on God! And that only leads to feelings of anger and bitterness, as they already know. When, in their frustration, they started to make demands on themselves, asking what they did wrong, they opened themselves to feelings of guilt and depression.

Positive Self-Talk, the kind that releases faith, focuses on the nature of God and his faithfulness. Clearly there are some events, some pain, some suffering that will come into our lives in spite of our words or our thoughts. Self-Talk is not some magic formula that can place God at our beck and call. When we keep the power of Self-Talk in its proper perspective, it provides us with the means to change our emotions and our behavior—regardless of the circumstances. Then we are open to the loving care of a sovereign God and can be at rest.

Questions for Personal Growth and Discussion

1. What demands do you sometimes make on God?
2. What specifically does it mean to you to rest in faith?
3. Think about what change would take place in your life this week if you allowed God to act creatively instead of expecting him to act on demand. How would that affect you?

TWELVE

Self-Talk and Self-Control

Rejoice always!

1 Thessalonians 5:16

Once we have found a balance point for our understanding of Self-Talk, the problems aren't completely resolved. Many people still question the basic idea that we can have control over our emotional and behavioral responses to life. We somehow think it has to be more complex or difficult. Using Self-Talk to create change is too simple.

Self-Talk Feels Phony

Our concerns can be expressed in several forms. One of the more common questions about Self-Talk relates to the statement that Self-Talk can't work because it feels so phony. And if you don't anticipate this potential roadblock, it is easy to give up working at changing your Self-Talk.

The fear that Self-Talk is phony is easy to understand. It feels as if we are trying to pull ourselves up by our own bootstraps. What is overlooked in this fear is the fact that Self-Talk is occurring all the time. The emotions and feelings you are experiencing as you read this page are a result of your Self-Talk. What we must always remember about Self-Talk is that we do not create it; we simply recognize that it is already there. The challenge is to learn how to change our Self-Talk and point ourselves in the direction of positive growth.

Whenever we attempt to change patterns of thinking it is hard work. We would rather stay as we are than make the effort required to change. And basically, we really don't like to change. It's like shopping for a new pair of shoes when the old ones are so comfortable. The new shoes fit, but they are so stiff. They don't feel like the old shoes. But we start wearing the new ones, and with time they start to soften and adjust to our feet. Soon they feel better than the old shoes.

The same is true with changing your Self-Talk. The new patterns may feel uncomfortable at first, but once you get into the habit of guarding your thoughts and your words, it becomes a way of life. To slip back into the old belief systems will, at that point, be as uncomfortable as the first steps in positive Self-Talk. Just keep at it! Very soon positive Self-Talk will begin to feel comfortable and genuine. At the same time you will be releasing a power for change that God has placed within you for your benefit.

But It Didn't Work

Another questioning statement commonly heard goes something like, "I tried it, but it didn't work!" Perhaps you've done each of the exercises suggested in this book, yet you are still fighting within yourself, trying to regain self-control. You may even be wondering why you've kept reading this far.

That's like those who start to exercise. They go to the gym for a couple of weeks, or they try jogging a couple of mornings, and then quit. They say, "I tried, but it didn't do any good!" In the area of physical fitness, evidence shows that the effects of exercise upon the body wear off within three days. Exercise must become a way of life if it is to affect the body.

We often have the same attitude about vitamins and the habit of good nutrition. We get all charged up after hearing someone explain the effects of vitamin and mineral supplements and healthy food in our diet. We go out and almost buy out the vitamin store. With enthusiasm we take everything recommended. Then two weeks later we get a cold, put the vitamins up in the cupboard, and say, "I tried it, but it didn't work." We overlook the evidence that the real benefits from vitamin and mineral supplements, along with good nutritional habits, come over a period of time, not immediately.

Just as exercise and good nutrition must become a way of life, so must positive Self-Talk. Usually we give up something because of some discouragement. We stop exercising because a muscle hurts. We quit our vitamin program because we get a cold. And we quit working on our positive Self-Talk because we don't see any quick changes.

When people return to my office with the statement, "I tried and it didn't work," I usually ask them a question: "What are you doing to prevent it from working?"

Usually the cause of the problem can be reduced to one of four reasons: (1) Either we are not taking the time to identify the demands we are making on ourselves and others; (2) we are holding on to irrational beliefs that we continue to choose to believe in spite of the contrary evidence; (3) we are not questioning and arguing within ourselves against these demands and/or irrational beliefs consistently enough; or (4) we have not spent enough time understanding our family of origin and the patterns of distorted Self-Talk we continue to use.

It takes time and effort to capture our thoughts and bring them into subjection. The suggestions in these chapters are just starting points. In order to keep from slipping back into old patterns, a lot of effort and time will be spent overcoming belief systems developed through the years. The payoff is worth the effort! Positive Self-Talk will lead to self-control.

If you are still struggling with identifying the problems in your present Self-Talk, try this. Ask what you were telling yourself just as you got angry. Or ask yourself what you were saying in your mind just before you felt those pangs of guilt or that panicky feeling of fear and anxiety. Identify what you said in your Self-Talk as you began to worry.

If you will identify these self-statements, take the time to write them down, and look within your family of origin for the roots of these self-statements, you can and will be able to capture your thoughts, change your emotions, and progressively experience more self-control.

Positive Change Can Occur

Each of the people we met in the first chapter had inaccurate perceptions of reality. Woven through Donna's belief systems were several phobias, anxieties, and fears. Donna could modify her emotions by gradually changing her belief systems. The starting point was to work on her fears.

Fred willingly offered to work with Donna to help her find ways to face her fears rather than give in to them. As she did this, she gradually became aware of a much deeper fear. She was afraid that if Fred became too successful, he wouldn't really need her. So Fred began to change his behavior by changing his Self-Talk. He started thinking and saying things like:

> I want to help Donna, and I can reassure her in positive ways of my love for her.
>
> I think I'll call Donna and let her know I'm thinking about her.
>
> I'm going to carefully monitor my actions to see if there are other ways I might be contributing to Donna's feeling of insecurity.
>
> I want to find new ways to let Donna know she is top priority with me.

As Fred worked on his belief systems, Donna began the process of restructuring her thought patterns—her Self-Talk. She started thinking and saying things like:

> Go ahead, fear, do your stuff. I'm not afraid of you anymore.
>
> I can focus on the ways Fred loves me, and that helps change my feelings of insecurity with him.
>
> I'm going to go early to church, sit in the middle, and before anyone else comes, see how serious my fears are. Fred will be there to help me.

Of course, Donna had to take a lot of other steps before she could free herself from her fears. But with Fred's consistent support, she has overcome her phobias and today enjoys her new way of thinking and living.

Marge stopped her out-of-control feelings by gradually telling herself things like:

> I don't have to do all the wash today. I can do just one load of wash and that will help.

I can be firmer with the kids. It may take some time before they really believe me. But I can handle that.

I wish I could listen to everyone's problems, but I don't have that much energy. I'm going to tell them when I feel overwhelmed by their problems.

Peggy is learning how to listen to other people. She's also discovering that it's OK to take care of herself as well as everyone else. She's changing her Self-Talk to sound more like this:

I really am efficient. So I don't have to be this busy.

I said no to that committee and the world didn't stop. I do have the right to say no.

It's usually been hard for me to slow down, but I am beginning to enjoy that process. I think I'll go explore those quaint little shops I saw last week.

Arnie finally agreed to look at his feelings about his son. He saw that not only was he overcontrolling his painful feelings related to his son but also was overcontrolling every positive emotion and feeling available to him. So he started to gradually change his Self-Talk to something like:

It's OK for me to hurt over my son.

I wish I knew where he was.

I'm really afraid of all this anger and guilt I feel, but I will survive better by examining these feelings rather than denying them.

It's hard for me to stop making demands on my son in my thoughts, but as I stop those demands, I am able to see some of his pain and fear.

It scares me to talk about these feelings, but I want to share this pain with my wife.

Obviously, these examples are only beginning steps for each person. But the principles of Self-Talk are clear and simple enough that almost all of us can start the process of positive change in our lives. Sometimes it helps to have the support of someone we can trust as we face ourselves and restructure our belief systems. That someone can be a professional counselor, a pastor, or a good friend.

The process of change is like running a race. When we enter the race, Paul says, we are to run as he does: "Forgetting what lies behind and straining forward to what lies ahead, I press on toward the goal for the prize of the upward call of God in Christ Jesus" (Phil. 3:13–14). Break with the patterns of the past, he urges. Instead, we are to strain forward—to reach for new goals and objectives.

In 1 Corinthians 9 Paul refers to the fact that, in a race, everyone competes but only one can win the prize. But the exciting thing about the "race of life" is that we can all win! We can all experience joy and satisfaction in living. The chief factor is in the training. That's why Paul adds, "Every athlete exercises self-control in all things" (v. 25). Paul wants us to train our minds and our belief systems much like an athlete trains for a race. And the fruit of that training is self-control.

The writer to the Hebrews sets up the race in an arena "surrounded by so great a cloud of witnesses, [so] let us lay aside every weight, and sin which clings so closely, and let us run with perseverance the race that is set before us, looking to Jesus the pioneer and perfecter of our faith, who for the joy that was set before him endured the cross, despising the shame, and is seated at the right hand of the throne of God" (Heb. 12:1–2). We run our race successfully by following the example of Jesus. He is the perfecter of our faith. He shows us by his attitude how we are to live. As we consider Jesus, we see him enduring hostility and the cross. He could do this because in his mind he focused on the joy that was set before him.

As a believer, by carefully focusing your thoughts you can release God's power within you, which will enable you to endure anything, face any fear, resolve any anger, renounce every worry and anxiety, survive any stress, and discover the joy of life.

Because our thoughts create our emotions, Paul can say to the people in Philippi, "Rejoice in the Lord!" That's why he can command the Thessalonians to "Rejoice always!" How can someone tell us to rejoice unless we have the ability to direct our thoughts and choose that attitude? Paul can say that because we do have that ability!

That's also why Jesus can say to the disciples, "This I command you, to love one another" (John 15:17). Because we are able to create our emotions by focusing our thoughts, he can command us to love.

When we don't feel loving toward someone, we can argue and dispute with our thoughts and belief systems that are causing us to feel unloving. Then we can, by guarding our thoughts and our words, change our emotions and experience love.

When someone comes into my office and shares with me that he doesn't love his wife anymore, I say something like, "That's interesting, but what difference does it make?" Then I go on to explain that if he doesn't love his wife anymore, the cause for those unloving feelings rests totally within him—in his Self-Talk. Quite often, in these cases, an amazing thing happens. People begin to see and understand that their thoughts create their emotions. And changing their thoughts by focusing on ways they can love their spouses, they actually begin to love their spouses again. Emotions can be changed!

So when that out-of-control world around you begins to press in and threaten your inner world, take control of your Self-Talk. Capture every thought. Argue and dispute with your irrational belief systems. You will be releasing powerful emotional energy within you as you let the presence of God work in your life. Then you will find yourself saying:

I can resolve my anger by identifying the demands I am making on other people, on God, or on life. Then I can change my Self-Talk by changing these demands into wants, wishes, and desires.

I can relieve guilt by examining areas of my life where I struggle with guilt. Then I can erase that guilt by focusing my Self-Talk on forgiveness.

I can be free from depression by identifying the demands I am making on myself. Then, through my Self-Talk, I can change these demands into wants, wishes, and desires.

I can eliminate worry and anxiety by looking for the demands I am placing on the future. I focus my Self-Talk on the trustworthiness of God—the only One who controls the future.

I can face the fears in my life by moving boldly against those fears, challenging them in my Self-Talk. Then I replace those fears with affirmations of courage and faith.

I can turn stress into a source of strength through my Self-Talk. I use the stress to my advantage by focusing my thoughts on God's ability and strength made available to me.

I can live assertively by releasing the emotion of love in my relationships. I remove the potential emotions of anger and fear through capturing my thoughts, then focusing my Self-Talk on love.

But where will you begin? The next step is the same as the first step—you begin by capturing every thought and bringing it into obedience to Christ. You'll notice that all seven points begin with the words *I can*. Life-changing Self-Talk always begins with the I can. The I can always leads you to the I will! The I will looks like this:

I Increase my self-control through positive Self-Talk

W Work on this one area where I feel out of control

I Involve myself in this specific first step

L Learn to reinforce this first step by repetition

L Love the positive changes in my emotions and behavior!

Take some time now to identify that one area you will begin to work on, and then write out your first step. That step will be some form of change in your Self-Talk, either by restating, arguing, and disputing old belief systems, or creating new thought patterns for positive Self-Talk. Then follow Paul's advice in Philippians 4:8–9, 7 (TLB).

> Fix your thoughts on what is true and good and right. Think about things that are pure and lovely, and dwell on the fine, good things in others. Think about all you can praise God for and be glad about. Keep putting into practice all you learned from me and saw me doing, and the God of peace will be with you. . . . His peace will keep your thoughts and your hearts quiet and at rest as you trust in Christ Jesus.

Notes

1. *Changing Times* (June 1979).

2. Aaron T. Beck, A. John Rush, Brian F. Shaw, Gary Emery, eds., *Cognitive Therapy of Depression* (New York: Guilford Press, 1979), 14.

3. See David Stoop, *Hope for the Perfectionist* (Nashville: Thomas Nelson, 1986).

4. Sandra Blakeslee, "Tracing the Brain's Pathways for Linking Emotion and Reason," *New York Times*, 6 December 1994, B1.

5. Alec Wilkinson, "A Changed Vision of God," *The New Yorker* (January 24, 1994), 52ff.

Dr. David Stoop is the founder and director of the Center for Family Therapy. He is the author of more than twenty-five books, including *Forgiving What You'll Never Forget*. David and his wife, Jan, have coauthored books and lead worldwide seminars and retreats on topics such as marital relationships, parenting, men's issues, fathering, and forgiveness. They have three sons and six grandchildren. Learn more at www.DrStoop.com.

Find More Resources and Connect With

DR. STOOP
@ DrStoop.com

What do we do when confronted with the unforgivable?

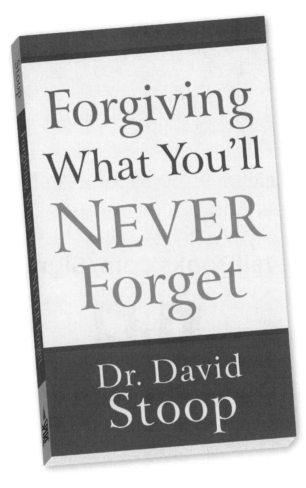

With deep compassion, clinical psychologist Dr. David Stoop shows readers how to reap the emotional and spiritual benefits of forgiveness, even when dealing with acts that seem unforgivable.